The Football Programme

The Football Programme

A History and Guide

John Litster

First published 2000, reprinted 2003, 2007

STADIA is an imprint of
Tempus Publishing Limited
Cirencester Road, Chalford,
Stroud, Gloucestershire, GL6 8PE
www.tempus-publishing.com

British Library Cataloguing in Publication Data.
A catalogue record for this book is available from the British Library

ISBN 978 07524 1855 1

Typesetting and origination by Tempus Publishing Ltd.
Printed and bound in Great Britain

Contents

Acknowledgements

This book has been written and illustrated from material gathered over thirty-five years of collecting and nearly twenty years of publishing *Programme Monthly & Football Collectable* magazine. The contribution of all those collectors and traders who have corresponded with the author over that period is gratefully acknowledged. A number of programmes were featured in 'Showcase' articles in *Programme Monthly*, which for some years were submitted by Roy Calmels of Sports Programmes, and Paul Clarkson of Matchday, whose assistance over the years is gratefully acknowledged.

Occasional passages of text have been adapted from articles submitted by collectors to *Programme Monthly* magazine and the specific contributions of the following are gratefully ackowledged:

Andy Porter (Spurs *v.* Old St Marks 1893)
J.S. Holmes (Manchester City *v.* Aston Villa FA Cup semi-final 1934; Newcastle *v.* York FA Cup semi-final 1955; England *v.* Wales 1937; England *v.* Austria 1932; England *v.* Ireland 1935)
Gary Spain (Scotland *v.* Ireland pre-war ; Hessen League *v.* League of Ireland 1950s)
Bob Grogans (Eyemouth United *v.* Celtic; Leith Athletic *v.* Rangers)
John Prince (Newcastle United Reserves *v.* Liverpool Reserves 1939)
John Holroyd (Nithsdale Wanderers *v.* Aberdeen)

One
The First Football Programmes

INTRODUCING FOOTBALL PROGRAMMES

Matchday programmes are unsurpassed as a medium of recording and reflecting upon the greatness of football. The triumphs and setbacks of the modern game are marked for posterity in their contents; the rich and varied history of football is best portrayed in nostalgic articles; and the game's personalities are profiled in words and pictures. For £1 or more, or even less at some non-League levels, programmes have an intrinsic, immediate value, unlike tokens such as stamps, coins and trade cards. Once the match is over, the publication which uniquely represented it takes on a different role and becomes 'a collectable'. In the years to come, it will also become a store of memories and nostalgia to football fans who can relive the roller coaster of emotions that make up a football season. It will remind readers of otherwise long-forgotten players, managers and personalities, and provide a valuable and authoritative historical and statistical chronicle of a period in a club's history. That same programme will have even further value to the owner if he or she purchased the programme at the match. In that context it will bring back memories of personal milestones, often during formative years. In a thriving second-hand market, the programme may complete a 'set' for an avid collector. This part of a programme's life introduces the whole ethos of programme collecting and the pleasure it brings to those who participate in the sense of achievement in building and completing sets, and who enjoy the friendships to be made throughout the country and overseas as one corresponds, exchanges, buys and sells with other collectors. Collecting programmes of other clubs and from other countries makes one realise the widespread popularity of our sport, and introduces the collector to other areas of his own country and those abroad.

Many youngsters learn their geography from a globe or atlas at home. If they are interested in football, they can use the hundreds of thousands of different football programmes to improve

Left: *It may look like an ordinary 1914/15 Manchester United issue, but this is the programme for the 1915 FA Cup final, in which Chelsea played Sheffield United at Old Trafford. At £11,500, this is believed to be the most expensive programme bought at auction. Right: In complete contrast, the 1970 World Cup finals tournament brochure featuring Brazil, arguably the greatest team in the history of the game, is readily obtainable at only £1.*

their knowledge of the geography of their country, continent and, increasingly, the entire world. Modern history – stretching back a century or more – is taught from books and videos, but the social fabric of a country and its interaction with other countries can be gleaned from the pages of football programmes. Advertisements give a good indication of the local economy, alternative forms of entertainment (with cinemas and theatres often being prominent advertisers in the past) and modes of transport. Editorial and player profiles also reflect contemporary society.

Thus football programmes are not just collectables. Most of them hold a powerful store of memories and history, and those twin features of football programme collecting will be described in this book. The development of the programme, from a simple team sheet used to identify players, to a glossy magazine, will form the basic thread of the narrative, interspersed with hints and tips on how to build up and store a collection of programmes, and descriptions of various programmes and their contents.

At the outset, it should be emphasised that this is not intended to be a definitive encyclopaedia of football programmes – such a work would be an enormous undertaking, given the range and diversity of programmes issued over the decades. Anyone wishing a closer study of the hobby, or wider coverage of specific examples, is referred to the final chapter 'Do You

Want to Know More?'. The intention of this book is to illustrate the fascinating history and information contained within programmes and demonstrate how a large and varied collection may be easily accumulated at little cost. Older, rarer items are detailed for those who may aspire to owning them one day and it is hoped that within these pages the flavour of the hobby will be imparted, demonstrating the enjoyment that can be derived from programmes and programme collecting.

THE EARLY FOOTBALL PROGRAMMES

Today's newspapers and magazines may use modern colour print and photographic techniques, but they would still be recognisable to a Victorian transported by time-travel to the present day. It is a similar case with other periodicals, and certainly with books. It is most unlikely, however, that our time-warped visitor would recognise the printed word as sold to him at a football match. The matchday programme has undergone dramatic change since it first emerged as a means of identifying players in the 1870s. Today, it is a glossy, colourful and sophisticated communications and marketing vehicle, sold in prodigious quantities and for sums far removed from the halfpenny or penny of the nineteenth century.

Thorne's Toffee dominates this Leeds United programme of 1929/30.

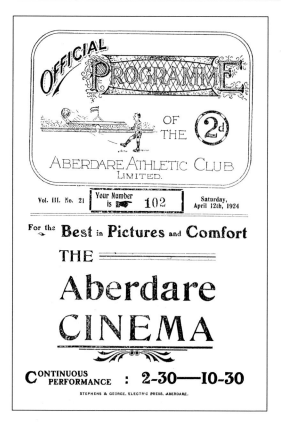

The local cinema takes pride of place on the front of this Aberdare Athletic programme of 1923/24.

Avid readers of modern programmes may bemoan the prevalence of advertisements, but these vital fund-raisers become fascinating historical markers as we roll back the years. The local butcher, baker and candlestick maker were present in just about every club programme, as was the local brewery, theatre (and later cinema), newspapers and menswear shops. The Halifax programme of 1937/38, for instance, was the usual mixture of adverts and basic features for the standard charge of 1d, with the front cover dominated by an advert for 'Yorkshire's Most Popular Beer'.

Local industries were prominent amongst the advertisements – razor blades in the Sheffield clubs' programmes, vehicle and cycle accessory manufacturers in Birmingham clubs' issues, shipbuilders advertising for workers on Clydeside. We can watch local economies evolve over the life of a club's matchday programme by reading the adverts. Trends within the game are, of course, apparent in editorials and features, while great teams, marvellous players and some unhappy times in the game may be recalled from the playing and managerial personnel listed in the programmes.

If the content of programmes down the years is varied, then so are the formats and styles used by clubs and associations. From the simple teamsheet of Victorian days, listing players and their distinguishing features, to the colourful, glossy booklets of the 1990s, the history of football programmes is as varied and interesting as the game itself.

Nineteenth-century team sheets

The first ever football programme is probably lying undetected in an old suitcase in an attic, or lining an antique cutlery drawer. It may even be displayed in one of the football museums which are springing up at clubs around the country. Quite frankly, no one knows which was the first ever fixture to have a team sheet printed and distributed to spectators, but we can take a pretty educated guess at how it looked.

The purpose of the earliest programmes was to identify the players and advise spectators of forthcoming fixtures. There were no team numbers on the backs of Victorian football shirts, but players did sometimes have distinguishing features, whether in the colour of their stockings or the type of cap or cowl they wore. Certainly there were well-defined formations – firstly 2-2-6 and then 2-3-5 – and spectators were able to identify the players from the positions they took up on the field, which corresponded to the formation in which their names were printed on the team sheet.

Thus, for the match between Queen's Park and The Wanderers on 9 October 1875, the home team's 'centre back-up' (centre half), C. Herriot, was to wear a 'Black and white cap – no stocking' while C.W. Alcock, the Wanderers captain and centre would wear a 'Cap – blue and white chequers'. The front of this card would be recognisable as a programme or team sheet today – it had the teams, referee and umpires and fixture details. If there was printing on the

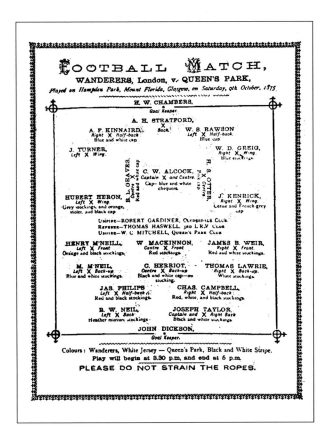

Team sheet issued by Queen's Park for the visit of The Wanderers to the first Hampden Park on 9 October 1875.

reverse, it would probably be a fixture list, perhaps incorporating results to date and details of forthcoming matches.

When Heart of Midlothian visited Royal Arsenal at Plumstead on 30 March 1891, the large single sheet had match details and team selections on one side, and on the reverse was printed a poem, which served as a welcome to the visitors. At the foot of the page were four small advertisements for local traders.

The first Tottenham Hotspur programme is thought to be for a London Senior Cup replayed tie between Tottenham Hotspur and Old St Marks, and is dated 28 October 1893. Andy Porter, the Spurs historian, advises that Old St Marks were an old boys team attached to St Marks College, Battersea. They won the replay 6-1 following a goal-less game (also at Tottenham) the previous week, Briggs scoring the goal for Spurs. 'A. Shooter' was a man named Bowyer who made his one and only senior appearance in a Tottenham shirt that afternoon. Otherwise, the Spurs line-up was as per the programme. One of the linesmen, H.D. Casey, was a founder member of the 'Hotspur FC' in 1882; they became Tottenham Hotspur FC in 1884.

In April 1893, at the Ardwick Ground on Hyde Road, Manchester (home of the club which evolved as Manchester City), Bolton Wanderers and Newton Heath (now Manchester United) contested a Manchester Senior Cup final and the team sheet, which sold for 1d, listed the teams with spaces to record the result and goalscorers. Much further south, Corinthians issued a single sheet, printed in red and black, for the visit of Sunderland to the Queen's Club, West London, in February 1898.

Royal Arsenal v. Heart of Midlothian.

Plumstead, March 30th, 1891.

ROYAL ARSENAL.

Goal.
BEE

Backs.
CONOLLY   COLLINS

Half Backs.
JOHNSTONE   STEWART   JULIAN

Forwards.
Right   *Centre*   *Left*
CHRISTMAS   HOWAT   BARBOUR   GLOAK   WOOD

HEART OF MIDLOTHIAN.

Goal.
FAIRBAIRN

Backs.
ADAMS   GOODFELLOW

Half Backs.
BEGBIE *Capt.*   MACPHERSON   HILL

Forwards.
Right   *Centre*   *Left*
TAYLOR   MASON   RUSSELL   SCOTT   BAIRD

Arsenal were south of the river (and Royal) when they entertained Hearts at Plumstead in March 1891 and issued this team sheet.

Spurs' first programme was issued 'gratis'. Spectators had to pay 1d after this issue.

As the game developed around the turn of the century, so did its programmes, and as football left the Victorian age, match programmes assumed some of the familiar features by which we recognise them today.

Collecting Tips: Buying these old items

Programmes such as those described above are, by dint of their age, extremely rare. On very few occasions will a nineteenth-century programme appear in a dealer's catalogue or in an advertisement within the pages of specialist magazines, such as Programme Monthly & Football Collectable, inviting offers. More usually, such items will be auctioned by a major auction house such as Christie's, Bonham's, Sotheby's and Phillip's.

Christie's were first to recognise the growing market for football memorabilia when they established an annual sale in Glasgow in 1989. Programmes were an important part of that sale, although they now assume a more subordinate role with a succession of famous footballers' caps, medals, jerseys and other memorabilia. The Christie's sale has now moved to London and is staged at least twice a year, while the other major houses have also established auctions throughout the country. Provincial auction houses, such a Vennett-Smith in Nottingham and Mullock Madeley in

Shropshire, have also established regular auctions of sporting memorabilia, with programmes prominent in each sale.

Details of these sales are advertised in specialist magazines, and catalogues may be purchased from the auction houses or downloaded from the relevant internet sites. Bidding may be done in person, by telephone, or 'by commission' by instructing the auction house accordingly. Bear in mind that a buyer's premium (usually 15 per cent) is added to the hammer price of the item, and if you are selling an item by auction the auctioneer will also deduct a seller's premium.

Some prices realised at auction as the twentieth century drew to a close included:

£11,500	*FA Cup final, Chelsea v. Sheffield United at Old Trafford, 1915. (This item cost £6,900 at an earlier auction.)*
£8,000	*Manchester United v. Queens Park Rangers, 1909.*
£6,700	*World Cup final, Italy v. Hungary, 1938.*
£6,100	*World Cup finals programme/brochure, Italy, 1934.*
£5,800	*Manchester United v. Wolves, 1958. (This was a match that was not played on the Saturday after the Munich Tragedy – only a handful of programmes survived.)*
£5,200	*Newton Heath (now Manchester United) v. Walsall Town Swifts, 1890.*
£4,600	*England v. Ireland at Trent Bridge, Nottingham, 1897.*
£4,300	*World Cup finals programme/brochure, France, 1938.*
£3,000	*Tottenham v. Arsenal, single-sheet emergency issue, January 1963.*
£2,200	*FA Cup final, Newcastle United v. Aston Villa, 1924.*
£1,900	*Red Star Belgrade v. Manchester United, February 1958.*
£1,900	*FA Cup final match card, Preston NE v. West Bromwich Albion, 1888.*
£1,900	*FA Cup semi-final, Bolton v. Sheffield United at Old Trafford, 1923.*
£1,700	*RSC Anderlecht v. Manchester United, 1956. (United's first European tie.)*
£1,700	*Manchester United v. Woolwich Arsenal, 23 November 1907.*
£1,600	*England v. Ireland at Middlesbrough, 14 February 1914.*
£1,600	*Huddersfield v. Sheffield United, FA Cup semi-final at Old Trafford, 1928.*
£1,400	*FA Cup final, Tottenham v. Wolves, 1921.*

Bound volumes of a complete season's programmes have also realised large sums at auction:

£6,100	*Sheffield United 1911/12*
£5,600	*Tottenham Hotspur 1914/15*
£5,500	*Manchester United 1936/37*
£3,300	*Tottenham Hotspur 1912/13*
£3,000	*Chelsea 1913/14*
£2,900	*Aston Villa 1906/07 (First season of the* Villa News and Record*)*
£2,600	*Sheffield United 1912/13*
£2,600	*Tottenham Hotspur 1913/14*
£2,300	*Sheffield United 1900/01*
£2,200	*Tottenham Hotspur 1927/28*

The 1900s and the first recognisable programmes

Programmes started to adopt something approaching their modern appearance when the clubs and authorities discovered that they could charge buyers a penny, thus introducing the possibility of the programme making a financial profit. To justify such a price they had to provide some value for money, which meant including more information on the club, their opponents and their respective players. Printers and publishers quickly cottoned on to the example shown by other branches of entertainment, chiefly the theatre, and attracted paid advertising to the issue. That, in turn, required sufficient sales to keep the advertisers happy, which meant that content had to be good enough to attract buyers at the match.

By this process, the match programme evolved from a single sheet, to a folded, and then stapled, publication. Liverpool first issued such an item in September 1892 with the visit of Rotherham Town to Anfield Road and their 1d programme was a four-page affair, with teams listed on the front page, surrounded by adverts, first and reserve team fixtures and results surrounded by adverts, and two pages of features on players, officials and recent matches, as well as a 'Notes' section.

The programme issued by Chester for the visit of Welsh club Druids on Christmas Day 1907 had the teams (in 2-3-5 formation) on one page, surrounded by adverts, and on the inside of the four-page folded programme was substantial editorial entitled 'Club Gossip', a

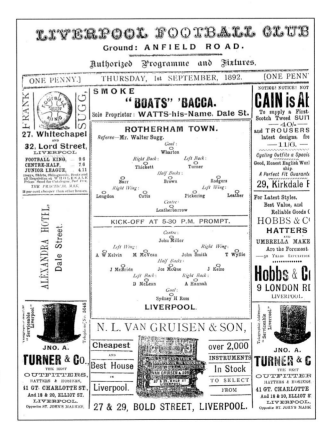

The Boer War – from which the Kop took its name – hadn't even started when Liverpool first issued a programme, against Rotherham Town in September 1892.

photograph and description on one of the home players, reserve team results and scorers, and 'Notes by Rambler'.

A number of clubs were more ambitious in their programme production. In 1887 Aston Villa entertained London Casuals and issued a 'Programme Card' but by 1906/07 they had launched *The Villa News and Record* in multi-page form **(see colour illustration 1)**. This remained at 1d, but sold far more copies than the brief team sheets of a few years previously, which in turn satisfied the multitudinous advertisers.

Not every League club issued for every fixture and it often took a special occasion to compel the club to print. One such milestone was Cardiff City's first ever match at Ninian Park, against Aston Villa in September 1910, and a special souvenir programme was issued, some time before City contemplated a regular programme.

The inexorable tide of commercialism was apparent even in those early days of the Association game and few clubs could resist the blandishments of advertising agencies and printers who put much needed money into club funds thanks to the penny programmes.

The programmes described so far, whilst extremely rare and much-coveted by collectors, are beyond the reach of all but a tiny minority of experienced and/or rich collectors. The beauty of programme collecting is that it is a hobby that can be greatly enjoyed without the expenditure of vast sums of money. Before we continue on our history of the development of football programmes, it is an appropriate time to remind ourselves of the joys of collecting and how to make a start in the hobby.

One large sheet folded into a four-page programme for Chester supporters in 1907/08.

Cardiff City issued a souvenir programme for the opening match at Ninian Park, against Aston Villa in 1910.

Collecting Tips: What's in a programme collection?

Every football fan who has bought and kept a match programme is in one of the four categories of programme collector – potential, latent, casual or confirmed. In the course of this book, it is hoped that those programme buyers from the first two categories will be converted into casual or confirmed collectors by describing the different types (sets) of programmes and by highlighting the pleasures that can come from collecting football programmes.

    A collection can be of any size, however modest or impressive, and can cost as much or as little as you want to spend on it. There are no barriers to entering the programme buying market and, therefore, you will find avid collectors from all walks of life. Subscribers to Programme Monthly *magazine, for instance, include solicitors, accountants, actors, schoolboys and girls, students, housewives, farm labourers, factory workers, teachers, business executives – and an MP from Mauritius. So it's not simply a case of 'You've bought the programme, now wear the anorak'!*

    'What do I collect' is not usually a question which arises in the early stages of a programme collection, which is first formed by the accumulation of programmes from various sources, mostly from the first few years of attending football matches. If the collecting 'bug' bites, then anything and everything will be voraciously added to a collection, and it is only when ambitions are limited by the availability of funds, that thought will have to be given to specialisation.

The composition of each collection is unique to its collector, so there are endless variations of collecting themes, but there are accepted basic building blocks. These will be described elsewhere in this book. As well as describing the 'sets', and the pitfalls and pleasures to be encountered en route, we will try to point out what to look out for in terms of value and collectability and perhaps give existing collectors – and those who accumulate programmes but don't consider themselves to be collectors – some ideas towards widening their horizons and deriving more pleasure from the hobby.

Many casual collectors will have a handful of 'landmark' programmes in their possession – cup finals and semi-finals (if their team has been fortunate enough to aspire to these heights), internationals, testimonials, special fixtures and major cup ties – each of which provides an interesting and achievable set to collect. Someone with a wider interest in football could collect other clubs, other leagues (perhaps venturing into non-League) or other countries – the possibilities are endless.

Collecting Tips: How to start a collection

One of the fascinating aspects of programme collecting is that no two collections are alike – each is unique to the individual collector, reflecting his or her footballing influences, matches attended and areas of special interest. Another feature of the hobby is that vast sums of money need not be spent – collecting football programmes can be tailored to anyone's age or budget. A programme collection can be of any

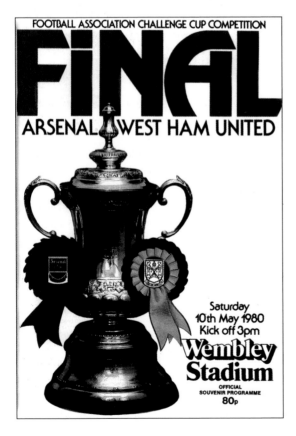

The most plentiful – and therefore cheapest – FA Cup final programme is the 1980 issue for Arsenal versus West Ham. You do not need to pay more than £1 for this item.

The Manchester United versus Tottenham Hotspur programme from November 1963 may be nearly forty years old, but United programmes are so plentiful that this one – featuring Law, Charlton, Greaves, White, Mackay and Blanchflower – can be purchased for about £1.

size – it can amount to tens of thousands of programmes accumulated over many years or it can comprise this week's and next week's issues on the way towards building a collection. If a journey of 1,000 miles starts with a single step, then a collection to be proud of starts with a single issue.

The obvious starting point is to retain programmes from matches attended. These will assume a greater importance in years to come because, as you review the hundreds or thousands of programmes, you can relate special personal memories to each of them. Friends and relatives will probably attend other matches, so why not ask them to buy an extra programme for you? Amongst friends and schoolmates, there will inevitably be others who share an interest in football and programmes. Swapping duplicated issues is another good way of adding to a small collection and this can be done by obtaining more than one programme from the matches attended, in order to exchange surplus copies for other match programmes. Exchanging a programme in your collection for another issue with a fellow collector can help towards building a set or speciality of programmes in your collection.

Every Saturday of every year, from August to mid-May, there are hundreds of senior football matches staged in the UK. Just about every one will have a programme issued, so the sky's the limit as far as items available for collection are concerned. Once the 'collecting bug' has bitten, the appetite for adding programmes to one's collection will be insatiable, but there is a limit on any new collector's budget, so specialisation is essential at an early stage of a programme collection. The most obvious, and most popular, is collecting programmes of a favourite team. The starting point would be immediate and henceforth an attempt should be made to obtain every home programme, with issues from matches not attended in person either obtained from the club shop or the club office. Programmes from away matches are another popular set and for both home and away collections you could go back to a certain date and attempt to collect back numbers. Those of a more recent vintage may be obtained from a club shop or a local programme dealer. The starting date can be variable – five years ago, ten years, from the date of the collector's birth, 1980, 1970, 1960, post-war and so on – another example of programme collecting's flexibility to suit any level of interest or any budget. One per club is an interesting early speciality, which involves an attempt to obtain one programme from every English League or Scottish League club, or both. Established collectors develop this into a 'one per club per season' collection. Those with an interest in non-League football can obtain a great deal of enjoyment from building a 'one per club' collection out of the thousands of different non-League clubs who have at one time or another issued a programme. Big match issues are a popular speciality and allow collectors to associate with the glamorous, high-profile matches in football history. Cup finals and semi-finals of either a domestic or European variety and programmes for internationals are obvious major categories for this type of collection.

Buying programmes at matches attended and exchanging with friends are fine means of starting a programme collection, but will prove to be frustratingly limited for those who seek to expand their collections and complete their chosen sets. The hobby has several mechanisms to meet more exacting requirements by collectors. One of the most accessible, and longest established, is the club shop. Run either by the commercial department or the supporters' club, the souvenir shop most often has a programme section managed by an experienced collector who spends countless hours obtaining a wide variety of programmes for his local clientele. The best of these shops can be a rich and enduring source of almost every category of football programme. Programme fairs are arranged throughout the country on most Sundays and it is a good idea to watch for press advertisements and notices in your club programme which announce these events in your locality. In many respects, these are an extension of the club shop, enabling collectors to leaf through thousands of programmes brought along by stallholders, thus enabling them to add to their chosen speciality.

It is at programme fairs that collectors may purchase 'bargain bundles' – for instance ten League match programmes for £1 – without incurring the cost of postage and packing. Similarly, browsing through the 'bargain boxes' of cheap programmes is an excellent way of widening your collection without spending a fortune. If collectors are searching for an elusive issue, or a number of rare or obscure programmes, finding them at a club shop or programme fair is a little bit 'hit or miss', although the euphoria at obtaining a much-sought-after item, at a bargain price, at an unlikely source, is one of the finest feelings in collecting. Such searching is most usefully conducted through a selection of mail order catalogues issued periodically by programme dealers located throughout the country. These catalogues are listings of thousands of programmes of all categories and prices and the best of them will contain most programmes required by comparatively recent collectors wishing to complete their first sets. For details of how to obtain these catalogues, see the final chapter of the book, 'Do You Want to Know More ?'

Two
Programmes Go Big Time

The 'big match' programmes

Such a title may have been applied in the recent past to a televised League match on a Sunday, but in programme parlance it refers to a whole range of programmes which are widely collectable by supporters of any individual club. Within that range there are many different categories.

The simplest explanation or definition is that they are of interest to collectors and supporters irrespective of the clubs they follow. Cup finals are an obvious example, in particular FA Cup, Scottish Cup and League Cup, which the majority of collectors would aspire to collect, if not in total, at least back to a certain date. Some may widen this to include sponsored tournaments, such as the Autoglass Trophy, the former Full Members Cup and, going even further back in time, the likes of the Watney and Texaco Cups.

Those with a continental bent would wish to collect European Cup, Cup Winners Cup (as was) and UEFA Cup finals; others with a non-League interest would seek out FA Trophy and FA Vase finals, and the old FA Amateur Cup finals. Few would restrict their interest to the finals – semi-finals are also highly collectable 'big match' issues and have the added benefit of being more numerous and varied in style and production.

International fixtures come into this category, with collectors in the four home countries invariably amassing England, Scotland, Wales or Northern Ireland programmes respectively. Some collect all four and add Eire for good measure. A more specialist diversion are under-age internationals (under-21, youth and schools fixtures), and inter-league fixtures of a few decades ago and earlier.

The power of television has brought European club football to the forefront in recent years and supporters of many clubs collect programmes involving British clubs in Europe, home and away. This category benefits from a comparatively recent start date (the mid-1950s at the earliest) and is one of the most varied and interesting of all the sets to collect.

Any and all of these form interesting and fulfilling collections in their own right. By the disparate (and often world-wide) nature of many of the fixtures, the only source of the programmes is via programme dealers, either by post or in person at programme fairs. Dealers make a point of stocking big match issues, in the knowledge that they are popular with their clients, and that they have a higher historical value in years to come (compared with ordinary League match issues) and will therefore always be re-sellable. The better club programme shops also strive to obtain supplies of big match programmes for their customers.

Cup finals and semi-finals

There is no better medium for recording the big, set-piece events in the footballing calendar than matchday programmes. Hundreds of thousands of FA Cup final issues are produced every year with football followers and TV viewers anxious to obtain a highly specific souvenir of the highlight of the football season. It is a similar case with important League games, such as the Liverpool *v*. Arsenal and Spurs *v*. Arsenal 'deciders', to name but two, and for international matches at home and abroad. The FA Cup final, the big occasion of the English soccer calendar – and a fixture that is beamed by television around the world – results each season in the biggest print run (and sale) of any match programme. The FA Cup final programme outsells the match attendance by a factor of between three and four, and that is despite a steep escalation in the price of this programme over the last decade.

Few wishing to expand their collections beyond their favourite clubs will fail to add FA Cup finals to their 'wants', with the rich folklore that the fixture brings, and the vivid memories of recent contests in every football fan's mind. Thankfully, the huge print runs and 'retainability' factor of these issues means that just about every FA Cup final programme of the last thirty years may be obtained at a reasonable price: Everton *v*. West Brom in 1968 would cost just £2.50, Arsenal *v*. Liverpool 1971 £5, Arsenal *v*. West Ham 1980 £1 and Everton *v*. Manchester United 1985 £4.

It is when one collects back into the 1950s and earlier that supply and demand begin to conflict and the prices rise. Expect to pay no less than £15 for Bolton *v*. Manchester United in 1958, £25 for Manchester City *v*. Newcastle in 1955, £50 for Arsenal *v*. Liverpool in 1950 and £85 for Charlton *v*. Derby in 1946.

There are one or two exceptions to the trends outlined above. The first Wembley Cup final to require a replay saw Chelsea and Leeds United meet at Old Trafford in 1970. Host club Manchester United produced the programme and, while the print run was generous, it did not match the huge quantities of Wembley Saturday fixtures. As a result the replay programme now demands a price of £20, while the Wembley fixture fetches only £5.

Other comparative shortages are the 1993 Arsenal *v*. Sheffield Wednesday replay which sells for £10 (first game £5) and Nottingham Forest *v*. Spurs in 1991 (selling at up to £20). The 1996 final between two eminently collectable clubs in Manchester United and Liverpool resulted in a shortage of programmes immediately after the match, the sales at Wembley exceeding expectations and resulting in far fewer than normal being available by way of post-match surplus. Once programmes begin to filter back into the trade (through people unloading unwanted programmes to dealers or selling collections) supply should meet demand, although it will inevitably be one of the less commonplace of FA Cup finals in the years to come and that will be reflected in the price.

The more memorable Cup Finals, in playing terms, are in greater demand. Any collector with a sense of history will want a copy of Blackpool *v.* Bolton Wanderers in 1953, also known as the 'Matthews Final' (which would cost around £50), while Bert Trautman's heroics in the Manchester City *v.* Birmingham 1956 final would cost up to £20 to recall in programme form.

The 1923 'White Horse' final between Bolton and West Ham, the first at Wembley, is arguably the 'penny black' of programme collecting and now fetches offers in advance of £350. Like the famous stamp, there are rarer and more expensive equivalents, but the 1923 FA Cup final remains a sought-after item for the majority of big match collectors.

While the most important day in the English and Scottish football calendars has always been their respective FA Cup finals, for many decades the quality and frequency of its programmes were far behind those issued by clubs. Indeed, it was not until the late 1900s that the football authorities took some interest in FA Cup final programmes, having previously stood back while outside publishers 'sponsored' matchday issues.

A number of nineteenth-century Cup Final programmes were published by *The People* newspaper. Printed locally, these Crystal Palace issues comprised a folded sheet with advertisements on one side – *The People* newspaper being prominent and surrounded by sports outfitters – and team line-ups and more advertisements on the reverse. They were sold as being 'the only authorised programme' and so few have survived that they now fetch five-figure sums at auction.

Some doubts as to the 'only authorised' issue status of these programmes have been raised by the existence of another version of a 1901 Cup Final teamsheet. An 'Official Programme' for the Tottenham Hotspur *v.* Sheffield United match, in the shape of a 7' x 5' blue card, has survived. This version is devoid of advertisements and one wonders if it was purely distributed to VIPs, as opposed to being on public sale.

The team sheet for the 1904 'English Cup-Tie' between Manchester City and Bolton Wanderers listed the players in two columns, and numbered them (1 to 22), reintroducing the original concept of a match programme – the identification of players by spectators. Curiously, the reverse side displayed the same names and numbers in 2-3-5 formation, along with the note: 'Any alteration taking place in the Players' Names, a board will be sent round the Ground corresponding with numbers on card'. It must have been a particularly large board to be seen by everyone in the 61,300 crowd at the old Crystal Palace ground!

When Newcastle United played Bradford City at the Crystal Palace in the 1911 final, W.H. Smith & Sons issued a 'Souvenir Card' priced 1d. Colin Veitch of Newcastle United was photographed on the front cover of this large folded sheet, with the team lines (unnumbered, in 2-3-5 formation) on the inside pages along with advertisements for *The Yorkshire Evening Post Football Edition* which 'containing full report of the Cup Final, will be on sale to-night at King's Cross, St Pancras, Marylebone and Euston stations on the departure of special trains for the North.'

The refusal of the Football Association to become involved in programme production has not helped in resolving this unofficial or official debate nearly a century later. This is similar with programmes for representative and international fixtures, which were left to the host club.

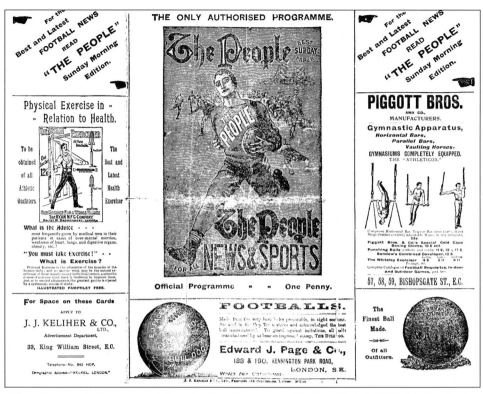

'The only authorised programme' from the Tottenham versus Sheffield United 1901 FA Cup final at Crystal Palace – although a single card issue has also survived.

It was not until the Cup Final moved to Stamford Bridge in 1920 that a single, definitive football programme began to be published for the fixture.

When Tottenham Hotspur met Wolverhampton Wanderers in the 1921 final, Chelsea issued a twenty-page programme on white paper. The outer cover, inside and out, was printed in blue, the inner pages in black. There was a full-page team group of each of the sides, and a full page was given to the photographs of the three match officials. Stamford Bridge final programmes were, of course, characterised by those splendid classical sketches by Bernhard Hugh, in which the mythical figure of Victory was joined by football items. In this case, it was the FA Cup itself, and a match ball. The programme was undoubtedly a substantial item for its time, and this was reflected in its price – 6d was a very high cost when the better League club programmes were selling for 1d or 2d.

How programmes developed following the Cup Final moving to Wembley in 1923 will be covered later in this book, suffice to say that all pre-war Wembley finals are very collectable, and some of them very expensive. Many football fans have vivid memories of a number of post-war FA Cup finals and the respective match programmes provide an enduring and appropriate souvenir of these occasions.

Arguably the most memorable of Wembley finals was the 'Matthews Final' of 1953, when the Blackpool winger at last crowned a magnificent career with his first domestic honour. It was very much a typical Wembley, (smallish) twenty-page, 1/-, programme which greeted the 100,000 crowd for the final, although the front cover, most unusually, featured only one colour, blue. The other two spot colours, green and red, were evident on the three advertising pages of the cover, but strangely not on the front page. There were portraits of the royal guests, a timetable of events and programme of music, and each team had four pages, two of pen pictures, a full-page team group and a lengthy article on the club and its history. Team lines were spread across the centre pages and a page and a half on notes from the cup's history completed an uninspiring production for an inspirational match.

Another memorable Wembley final was in 1981, when Spurs and Manchester City fought out a superb replay, crowned by a stunning winning goal for Spurs by Argentinian Ricardo Villa. The FA Cup final programme is the biggest and best produced in the UK every season and the sixty-four-page issue for the first match on 9 May 1981 was no exception, although it looks small and inconsequential compared with today's brochure-sized magazines **(2)**. The full colour production gave extensive coverage to both clubs and was particularly strong on articles on the history of the FA Cup.

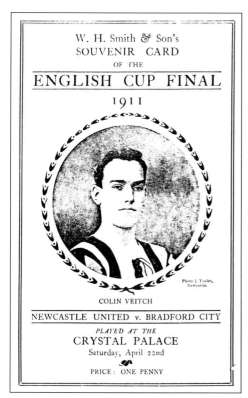

Left: W.H. Smith issued souvenir cards for FA Cup finals early in the twentieth century. This one from the Newcastle United versus Bradford City, costing one penny, is a fine example. Right: Tottenham versus Wolves in the 1921 FA Cup final at Stamford Bridge. Not only was this a substantial, recognisable programme in contrast to the team sheets previously issued, it was also acknowledged to be the only official programme for the fixture.

THE FOOTBALL ASSOCIATION CHALLENGE CUP COMPETITION

FINAL TIE

BLACKPOOL v BOLTON WANDERERS

SATURDAY, MAY 2nd, 1953   KICK-OFF 3 pm

EMPIRE STADIUM

WEMBLEY

Chairman and Managing Director :   SIR ARTHUR J. ELVIN, M.B.E.

OFFICIAL PROGRAMME · ONE SHILLING

This rather plain cover introduced the programme for the 'Matthews Final' in 1953.

The printers had only five days to prepare the replay programme, which was understandably smaller, at thirty-two pages, and cheaper at 60p **(3)**. Two-page spreads of both team groups were included for the first time, along with some new features, plus half a dozen pages of pictures from the drawn match. There were no pen pictures, but the full colour programme was an excellent effort in such a short space of production time. The programme from the first match is plentiful and can be purchased for between £1 and £2. The replay – Wembley's first – is slightly more scarce, but there are sufficient on the market and may be purchased for between £1.50 and £3.

By 1987, and Coventry City's remarkable 3-2 victory over Tottenham Hotspur at Wembley Stadium, the producers of Cup Final and international programmes were favouring brochure-sized issues and there was plenty of colour in the £2 programme, which sported a high-gloss light card cover **(4)**. The sixty large pages gave ample scope for expansive features on the clubs and the occasion, and there is no doubt that modern Wembley programmes of this style are fitting souvenirs of major football matches. Contents included Cup Final memories by Kenneth Wolstenholme, players from both squads describing their musical tastes, a feature on Cardiff's FA Cup victory sixty years earlier and extensive coverage of the competing clubs, their players and route to the final. The programme cost double the cover price of club issues of the time, but it represented value for money in terms of content and presentation, and of course as a unique souvenir of the occasion. Most FA Cup final programmes over the last thirty-five years were produced in enormous quantities and this one is obtainable at little more than its original cover price.

Two years later, Liverpool and Everton matched the 1987 scoreline in a dramatic all-Merseyside final. Wembley's brochure-sized big match programmes were well into their stride by 1989 and the £3 issue for the Cup Final weighed in at 108 pages, in full glossy colour with a high-gloss light card cover which featured one of the twin towers **(5)**.

Contents included historical articles on past finals, 'The Changing Face of Wembley', star players over the years for both finalists, the competing managers (Colin Harvey and Kenny Dalglish), players who missed out on past Cup Finals and fourteen pages of results from that season's competition, starting from the Preliminary Round on 3 September (Esh Winning 1 Ryhope CA 1, watched by 30 spectators), illustrated with Player's Cigarettes FA Cup winners cards. There was also extensive coverage of the competing clubs, their players and their route to the final, and the entire production resembles a brochure rather than a programme or even 'match magazine' as many are labelled. Unfortunately, the large number of pages gives scope for many advertisements to be included and this issue is particularly heavy in that regard.

Cup semi-finals form a varied and interesting big match collection, and are of particular interest with regard to those quickly forgotten teams – the beaten semi-finalists. Birmingham *v.* West Brom (1968), Leicester *v.* Sheffield United (1961), Burnley *v.* Fulham (1962) and Preston *v.* Swansea (1964) are, with respect to the clubs involved, unlikely semi-final pairings in today's game, but the programmes from these fixtures can be picked up for a few pounds each and faithfully record the Cup aspirations of the clubs. In Scotland, just about every present day First and Second Division club has reached the semi-finals of one of the two national cup competitions within the last thirty years, and programmes are readily available to testify to such flirtation with glory.

Stamford Bridge may have lost the Cup Final to Wembley in 1923, but it did host one of the semi-finals, and Chelsea issued a familiar four-page issue (of *The Chelsea FC Chronicle*) for the meeting of Derby County and West Ham. In truth, there was as much to read in this compact, advert-free large folded sheet as there were in many contemporary multi-page productions – and there was the added bonus of the excellent cartoon on the cover.

An example of a small club having its 'day in the sun' was the Newcastle *v.* York City FA Cup semi-final replay on 30 March 1955. This was the first-ever all-ticket game at Roker Park, when a semi-final (albeit a replay) came to Sunderland, and a programme of (approximately) 8.5in x 5.5in was produced with a front cover containing plenty of red colouring, an advertisement for a well-known brewery and a sketch of the ground, with excellent green contrast for the pitch – but why was the far goal set up in the first row of the terrace and the arc to the penalty area missing, even though it was introduced in the 1937/38 season? Costing three old pence, sixteen pages included the team line-ups on the inside of the front cover, with the middle two pages comprising a block which gave the progress of both clubs to the semi-final, surrounded by advertisements, and there were six other full pages of advertisements – the programme containing a total of seven for beers, wines, spirits or soft drinks. One page of Sunderland FC's fixtures for the season (with results up to date), a page and a half for 'The Editor's Review', and pen pictures of both teams completed the reading matter. Not surprisingly, the notes about Jackie Milburn had as many lines as the combined total of four of the York team!

There are, of course, finals and semi-finals of other competitions, in addition to the FA Cup. Scotland (with three national cup competitions), Northern Ireland and Wales all have

West Ham versus Derby County, FA Cup semi-final at Stamford Bridge in March 1923.

their own national cups, while England has the League Cup, the Auto Windscreens Shield Cup (and its variously sponsored predecessors) and in the recent past the Anglo-Italian Cup, with area finals and national finals at Wembley. In the 1970s, there were Watney and Texaco Cup (later the Anglo-Scottish Cup) competitions, which produced interesting, varied and very collectable programmes.

Pre-war programmes

In terms of antiquity, programmes tend to be split into three time zones: post-1960, pre-1960 and pre-war. The 1960 divide may be movable with the passing years, as it marks a certain age when programmes cease to become commonplace in the market as those items which have survived three or more decades are taken out of circulation and into collections. At present, the 1960 benchmark is the dividing line between programmes that will be on 'straight sale' in a dealer's catalogue and those older items for which offers may be sought in a postal auction. As the years progress, it may be that this mark will move to around 1965, although it is difficult to imagine much scarcity of items from the late 1960s to the present day, with larger print runs and a greater awareness about the collectability of football programmes at the time of publication and matchday purchase.

A more natural, logical and fixed divide is the Second World War. It is within this six-year span from 1939 until 1945 that the biggest jump in programme prices is seen and it is exceptionally rare to see pre-1940 programmes being sold on the open market at fixed prices. There is some irony in this, as more copies of some pre-war programmes exist, than those for up to a decade later. The majority of Football League clubs issued substantial programmes, in size, pagination and content, in the 1930s. Immediately after the war, however, programmes were truncated in both size and circulation, due to paper being rationed. Not only were less programmes printed and purchased, but the inferior quality and paper has seen few survive the buffetings of the passing years.

Indeed, it took some decades before clubs restored their programmes to their pre-war glory. Programmes of twenty pages and more were common in the 1930s, but it took until the 'modern programme revolution' of the mid-to-late 1960s before that size and scope of issue was seen again. Many clubs, including some of the biggest in the country, were reluctant to improve on the 'penny dreadfuls' of the years of rationing, even when restrictions were lifted. Thus we find the marvellous Spurs double-winning side of 1960/61 commemorated by home programmes which consisted of no more than a folded sheet.

Pre-war programmes may cost a great deal of money, therefore, but they invariably prove to be sizeable issues with plenty of content pertaining to both the history of football and socio-economic history (through the obtrusive advertising). Their prices are escalating, aided by the increasing involvement of auction houses in their sale. In the majority of cases, it is programme

Spurs were only six home games away from the first league and cup double of the twentieth century when they played host to Sunderland in an FA Cup sixth round replay in March 1961, but they were still issuing the four-page (folded sheet) 2d issue of the previous fifteen years.

dealers who are bidding £50 and more per programme when, for instance, a dozen Arsenal issues of the early 1930s or a bound volume of Sheffield United programmes from the 1920s, come to auction. Dealers obviously expect to resell these items at a profit, which could mean final prices, through postal auctions, of up to £100.

It is most unlikely that anyone starting in the hobby will choose to specialise in pre-war; most collectors who concentrate on these items have been collecting for many years and accumulated their earlier programmes some decades ago. Alternatively, they may have exhausted their post-war collection and only pre-war programmes remain for them to collect.

MORE SUBSTANTIAL ISSUES BEFORE THE GREAT WAR

The fund-raising potential of football programmes became widely appreciated by clubs in the years which followed the turn of the century and, by the outbreak of the First World War, clubs had become polarised into those who published multi-page, advertising-included recognisable match programmes and those who published nothing at all. Few, if any, remained with the halfway house of a simple team sheet.

Some of those early programmes were lavish affairs, providing a comprehensive coverage of club matters, commentary on football topics and description of visiting clubs. *The Villa News and Record* comprised twenty pages and was arguably superior to the club's programmes some fifty years later **(1)**. Birmingham City (or just plain Birmingham as they were then known) favoured a very large page size, with a cover of blue paper and white internal pages **(6)**.

A curiosity amongst programmes from the early decades of this century was the *Everton and Liverpool Official Football Programme*, which was 'the only programme issued by Authority of the Everton and Liverpool Clubs'. This was a substantial, sixteen-page edition, which covered both city clubs, featuring the first team match of one, and the reserve team fixture of the other, both played on opposite sides of Stanley Park on the same afternoon. This (apparently) happy collaborative arrangement persisted for many years on Merseyside, before the clubs reverted to their nineteenth-century habit of issuing separate match programmes in the late 1930s. The cover illustrated here is from 26 August 1933, the first issue of the twenty-ninth season of this unique arrangement.

An earlier example of this programme is the Liverpool *v.* Birmingham City FA Cup-tie, played on 21 February 1920. This was Volume 16, No. 35 of the Everton and Liverpool joint programme, printed by the Programme Syndicate of Dale Street, Liverpool. At 8.5in x 5in, it was a smaller version than before the First World War, the programme increasing in size and content until 1939, although the clubs were publishing their own by then. With sixteen pages of black print on dull white paper, the programme carries not only football news from the city but theatre and film news and advertisements for taxis, tooth extraction by gas and Houldings Ales – a full day's entertainment, in fact! Indeed, adverts are on every page with text and information filling the centres. The second and third pages are taken up with the editor's comment on the Reds' seven consecutive wins and the Blues' recent draw at Aston Villa. Page five has the line-ups for Everton A's game versus Ormskirk & District. More Liverpool jottings follow on the next page with the Central League table on page seven, then a full page of advertisements with line-ups for the real match on the second centre page. Page ten has a

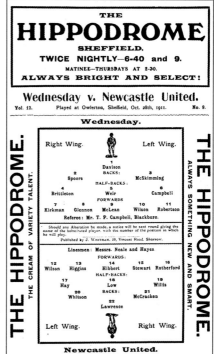

Left: The curious Everton and Liverpool programme, which ran for the first three decades of the twentieth century, to the apparent satisfaction of both clubs. Right: *Wednesday (without the Sheffield prefix) versus Newcastle United, October 1911.*

statistical piece about Everton and Liverpool wartime games, followed by the half-time scoreboard. Amongst the other seven ties played that day, Notts County played Bradford Park Avenue and Arsenal faced Manchester United. Pen pictures and 'Welcome to our visitors' take up small parts of the next two pages, with League Division One and Two and the Lancashire Cup on the inside back cover. News of pantomimes at the Empire and Olympia complete the programme.

The Sheffield clubs were early and prolific programme issuers, with Wednesday being one of the last clubs to feature team selections on the front page. Their sixteen-page productions from the early 1900s were arguably before their time, although they continued to have the team formations on the front page right up until the 1930s. Across the steel city, Sheffield United favoured ornate cover designs, skilfully incorporating front page advertisements, in their substantial issues from the early years of the century.

It was not only League clubs who were beginning to make their programmes bigger and better. Hartlepool United, who did not join the League until after the First World War, had 'Martin's Key Card and Official Programme' issued on their behalf as early as 1909/10. This consisted of twelve pages, only three of which were given over to advertisements.

By the outbreak of the First World War, those clubs who regularly issued programmes were publishing multi-page issues which we would recognise today – minus the gloss, colour and

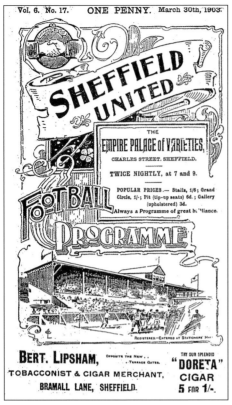

Left: *Sheffield United's attractive and ornate cover design from the 1902/03 season.* Right: *Hartlepool United, 1910/11.*

photography of course. Universal programme production across the country did not happen until the 1920s.

Everybody's doing it – the 1920s

Programme issuing by clubs and associations became the norm in the 1920s, resulting from the example shown by those clubs whose programmes before the First World War had proved to be good sellers, and highly profitable. Another reason for the explosion of issues was the widespread provision of half-time scoreboards around football grounds. In the days before radio coverage and teletext, football crowds had to rely on the half times from other grounds being displayed on enormous fixed boards (either at the back of the terracing or at the trackside), to ascertain how rivals were faring. The only means of deciphering the mixture of letters and numbers was to refer to the coded list of fixtures printed in the match programme. In this way, the programme had evolved from being merely a means of identification of players, to being a more sophisticated vehicle for greater spectator information.

Part of the sudden upsurge in programme production was the virtual doubling of the size of the Football League in the early 1920s, with the formation of Division Three (North) and the transfer of clubs from the Southern League to form Division Three (South). Thus we see the first regular issue of programmes from Rochdale in 1922/23, Halifax Town in 1921/22 and such long forgotten ex-League clubs as Wigan Borough and Stalybridge Celtic (both 1921/22) and Nelson (1924/25). Of clubs to join the League in subsequent years, York City issued an eight-page programme in 1923/24 in the Midland League, and Torquay United first issued (starting with FA Cup-ties) in 1923/24.

Chelsea, host club of the 1920, 1921, and 1922 FA Cup finals, set a fine example by publishing the first truly official, and substantial, FA Cup final programmes. Featuring classical sketches by Bernhard Hugh on the cover, these were twenty-four, twenty and eight-page programmes respectively, the last bearing a very close resemblence to the standard Chelsea programme of the inter-war years.

The 1920s was the decade in which football programme production became the norm throughout the Football League and for all major non-League clubs, and it was also the era in which programmes adopted the format we associate with them today. Henceforth, match programmes would be multi-page, stapled, liberally filled with advertisements and including as a minimum: team selections, fixtures and results, league tables, half-time scoreboard information and editorial.

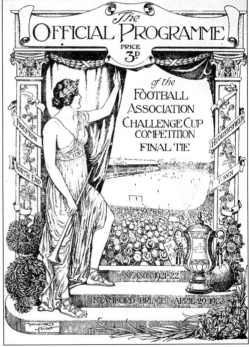

Left: *York City issued programmes for first team and reserve matches whilst in the Midland League in 1923/24.* Right: *Chelsea's issue for the 1922 FA Cup final between Preston North End and Huddersfield Town at Stamford Bridge. Note the elaborate cover sketch by Bernhard Hugh.*

Wembley and the advent of big match programmes

We have previously noted that the FA were reluctant to get involved in programme production for FA Cup finals, but that changed in 1923 when Wembley opened (albeit the publishers of Cup Final and international issues from that venue were the stadium authorities themselves with FA approval). The scale and design of these programmes matched that of the venue. For the first time, colour appeared on British programme covers and the contents were more substantial with photographs and greater coverage of players.

Wembley opened with the famous 1923 Cup Final and the programme for that fixture comprised twenty-eight pages, arguably the most published in a match programme to that date. It should be noted, in passing, that although this is possibly the most famous programme, it is by no means the rarest nor most expensive nor coveted. Indeed, the following year's final programme is far rarer and costs three times as much at auction.

Unusually, the programme was smaller than A5 in size, although the use of four colour artwork on the front cover was probably a first for a programme in this country. Four of the five opening pages were full-page adverts – Swan Fountpens, Reid's Stout, The Cup Safety Match and Huntley & Palmer's Cornish Wafers. Interrupting these were three photographs of the president, secretary and treasurer of the FA. A page with fixture details disclosed that the programme was published by W.H. Smith & Son, The Arden Press, Stamford Street, SE1, and

Not the 'Penny Black' 1923 cup final, but the far rarer 1924 tie, which featured Newcastle United and Aston Villa.

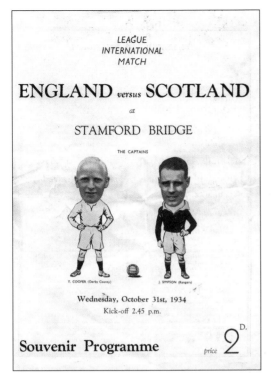

Left: *Unusually for Chelsea, this programme for the English League versus the Scottish League match in 1934 does not include a cartoon.* Right: *The 1928 FA Cup final featured Blackburn Rovers versus Huddersfield Town.*

while this is undoubtedly recognised as the official programme for the match, there were earlier finals in which Smith's were only one of a number of publishers of teamsheets and programmes.

Various Gibbs medications occupied a full-page advertisement, before two full pages on the history of the FA Cup. Officials and match details are on one page, then come full pages on Bolton Wanderers' history and pen pictures of the team. Centre fold are the team line-ups (in 2-3-5 formation) with a small advert for 'Steelwork, Booth, Bolton'. A full-page photograph of Bolton is opposite the remaining pen pictures, along with a note of how both teams reached the final. West Ham are then covered, in similar style, over three pages. There are five pages on the Empire Stadium and Exhibition, and the programme closes with adverts for Morris's Cigarettes, the Sheffield *Green 'Un* newspaper and Pinnace Cigarettes. On the back page is a four-colour advertisement for Meltis Chocolate.

Host clubs continued to issue programmes for FA Cup semi-finals and international and representative matches played at their grounds (until the 1950s the majority of England international matches were played on club grounds). Hitherto, the clubs had merely issued similar, if not identical, programmes to their standard League issues, but the example shown by Wembley spurred them into making a special effort for the big games entrusted to their care.

An example of this is Chelsea, who maintained the same four- or eight-page, blue-print-on-white-paper programme style until after the Second World War. In October 1934, they

Left: *The 1929 FA Cup final, Bolton Wanderers versus Portsmouth. The front cover design was in blue and salmon contrast, with the centre trophy in pale blue.* Right: *The 1933 FA Cup final, Everton against Manchester City, had a programme cover in green and black.*

staged the English League *v.* Scottish League match at Stamford Bridge and issued a special programme comprising the normal eight pages, but with photographs on the centre and front pages, and red print as well as the standard blue on the front cover. The price remained the standard 2d.

Wembley programmes were not only the first to use full colour, but they also saw a rich variety of programme designs. All of the pre-Second World War covers relied on sketches and graphics, with photographs used sparingly, and some of the full colour sketches were very attractive indeed. Almost all of them featured the 'twin towers' in some form or another, whether in a photograph (1925), logo (1935) or as background (1931 and 1933). Most years saw an advertisement at the bottom of the front page – either 'Drink Bovril. Once it's in you it's sinew' or 'Expert Criticism of today's cup tie by Charles Buchan in the *Daily News*' (or *News Chronicle*) (1928 and 1929).

The example set by Wembley ensured that from then on big match programmes would invariably fit the occasion they sought to represent and programme buyers could anticipate something superior to the normal League fare.

Three
Programmes Go International

International programmes

The varying fortunes of international teams, and international players, are reflected in the big match programmes produced for their fixtures, and the half dozen or so games played by each of the Home Counties each season form an easily collectable set. For current season programmes of this type, most club programme shops carry stocks and locally organised programme fairs are certainly a very good source. Most dealers also stock popular current season programmes. Ironically, despite the importance of the fixtures, copies of previous season big match issues may be picked up from dealers at a reasonable discount, or as part of bargain bundles. This is because the high match-day cover price (reflecting the sizeable nature of the productions) does not equate with the limited demand for these programmes a couple of years later. In terms of cost of older programmes, international prices are less steep than, say, Cup Finals and early 1960s programmes can be obtained for between £1 and £2, late '50s £3, early '50s £3 to £7. Pre-war and immediate post-war programmes are more expensive, and harder to collect items may only surface via offers lists, but for many programmes, prices can often be less than League match programmes of a similar vintage. Of particular interest, from the England team's point of view, are programmes for home games played at stadia other than Wembley. Examples include 1966 *v.* Poland at Liverpool, 1962 *v.* France at Hillsborough, and 1961 *v.* Luxembourg at Highbury and, indeed, all but the Scotland pre-war internationals were staged at London clubs or provincial grounds.

Programmes for all the Home Countries' matches abroad vary in scarcity. Some are extremely difficult to obtain and very obscure, particularly those for South American or Iron Curtain countries before 1970. Others, particularly in the last twenty years when

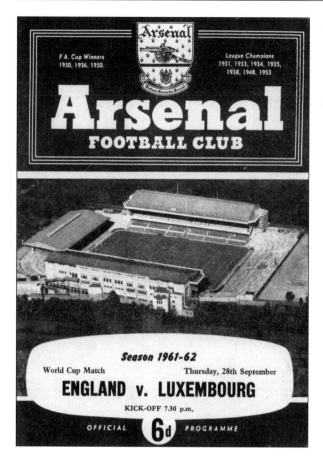

A World Cup qualifier between England and Luxembourg, played at Highbury. Arsenal issued their standard sixteen-small page programme of the time, with red and black on the front cover.

dealers imported in quantity, are rather more plentiful and are priced accordingly. Inter-League programmes (up to the early 1970s) are an interesting feature for those with a sense of football history, covering a four-way tournament most seasons between the Scottish League, English League, Irish League and League of Ireland (Eire). Under-21 (and their under-23 predecessors) and youth international programmes are interesting items to collect and reflect upon in later years, particularly in view of the subsequent careers of the players involved. A typical example of a provincial under-age tie occurred when Middlesbrough hosted an under-23 international between England and Scotland in March 1961 and used the rose and thistle to illustrate the two-colour cover (7).

Full internationals

Euro '96 illustrated the enormous interest that the international game can generate amongst British football fans, no matter what their preferences at club level; this is reflected in the popularity of international match programmes. The keenest of collectors accumulate issues from a number of countries (for example, all four home countries' matches, and perhaps those of the Republic of Ireland) although the majority restrict their interest to the country of their nationality.

Programme sales at international matches sometimes exceed attendances, illustrating that many programmes are 'brought back from the match' by friends and relatives. Not all collectors can rely on this personalised service, however, and the majority rely on programme dealers or shops. These traders are diligent in obtaining supplies of home and away international matches, either dealing directly with the football authorities, or relying on travelling fans returning with pre-ordered supplies. The cost of carriage is significant, however, leading to the cost to the collector being upwards of £4, irrespective of the cover price in the local currency. Mind you, that does compare well with the recent cost of Wembley international programmes, albeit that these matches see a superb, colourful, glossy programme produced.

Prior to 1950, few internationals other than the England *v.* Scotland clashes were played at Wembley, so club issues predominate for that period. Whereas pre-war England-Scotland programmes will fetch upwards of £100 at auction (such as the 1932 match), and much more than that for the Wembley meetings of the 1920s, matches against Ireland and Wales, and continental countries at Maine Road, Old Trafford, Hillsborough, Bramall Lane, Villa Park, Ayresome Park, Huddersfield and many more played at club grounds are perceived to be harder to obtain, and will attract more demand because of their novelty

A 1937 England international at Tottenham Hotspur's White Hart Lane. Note the prominence given to FA officials.

and club association. Matches staged in London, at Highbury and White Hart Lane, are more plentiful, but remain expensive and liable to come to the market either at auction or on dealers' postal offers lists.

Scotland's first visit to Wembley was on 12 April 1924, and a large-sized twenty-eight page programme was issued, with the front and back covers illustrated in four colours. The inside front pages were left blank, and page three carried match details with an ornate border design. There were full-page advertisements for Gibbs Cold Cream Shaving Soap, Sanitas Embrocation, *The Daily Mirror*, the Royal Tournament and, on the back page, Peak Frean biscuits. There were smaller adverts for Sunripe Cigarettes and *The Daily Chronicle*.

A full-page photograph of the Prince of Wales, president of the British Empire Exhibition which was the inspiration for the building of the stadium, was joined by four photographs to a page of FA and SFA officials, head-and-shoulders shots of all twenty-two players (spread over four pages) and three sketches of the Exhibition grounds.

The text includes a two-page article 'History of the International Game', two pages each are devoted to the teams' pen pictures, a list of previous fixtures, the programme of music and a page is given to the Empire Exhibition.

Programmes from recent England international matches are not difficult to obtain, if a little expensive at times only by virtual of the high original cover price. That also applies to the vast majority of international programmes from the last twenty-five years, although there are one or two rarities where match attendances perhaps exceeded expectations, leading to few surplus programmes, or for obscure away matches. The World Cup qualifier Poland *v.* England from October 1989 usually appears only on offers lists, while the home match *v.* Northern Ireland in 1974 costs around £6, compared with £1 for the home matches against Argentina and Czechoslovakia in the same years.

Collecting older international programmes is an interesting pastime, their contents being steeped in football history. Forty-year-old England programmes will have the names Mannion, Matthews, Finney and Wright prominent and, up until the mid-1960s, the majority of home matches were played on club grounds. The host club had responsibility for producing the match programme in these instances, and few deviated from their normal League styles. Thus we have England *v.* Wales at Maine Road in 1946 (offers over £50), England *v.* Switzerland at Highbury in 1948 (another offers item), the visit of Luxembourg to Highbury in 1961 (sale price £3) and France to Hillsborough in 1962 (approximately £7.50).

For Austria's first visit to England, in December 1932, a souvenir programme measuring 10in x 7.5in was produced for the game at Stamford Bridge. It cost three old pence and was published by the Chelsea programme printers of the time, Jas. Truscott & Son Ltd. A striking front cover, with blue print on a white background, gave details of the fixture, and there were large crossed flags (in colour) of the two nations, and a red horizontal stripe at both top and bottom. In addition, there were inset black and white photographs of the respective captains. The back cover set out the teams in blue print, with red horizontal stripes similar to those on the front cover.

There was a welcome, in both languages, to the visitors on the inside front cover, followed by a full-page photograph of King George V, the patron of the FA. Details of past games between the countries (all four played in Vienna) and details of some of the visitors

The FA took the Northern Ireland home international match to Goodison Park in November 1953, leaving Everton to modify their normal match day programme and cover design.

took up two pages, followed by photographs (by Wilkes of West Bromwich) of the England team on two pages. Photographs of the visitors in a similar style were on the next two pages. Pen pictures of the England team followed, and a contemporary photograph of a very open Stamford Bridge completed the programme with not an advertisement in sight.

By a strange twist of fate, both centre forwards on the programme that day died a few years later of unnatural causes – Jimmy Hampson of Blackpool, who scored twice in the match, was drowned whilst on a fishing expedition off Fleetwood in 1936 and Matthias Sindelar of FC Austria, said to be one of the most gifted Europeans between the First and Second World Wars, died in a gas-filled room in 1939.

For the England *v.* Ireland match on 6 February 1935, the Everton and Liverpool football programme had a small amount of colour (blue as the game was at Goodison) on the word 'Official' and the shirt and tops of the socks of the player in the action sketch on the front outer cover. Costing two old pence, the programme was about 7in x 9in. An inside front page relevant to the history of this particular fixture was followed by the briefest pen pictures of each player – only surname, place of birth, height and weight.

In comparison, the presidents of the respective Football Associations, president of the Football League, chairman and vice-chairman of the host club, and the secretary of the

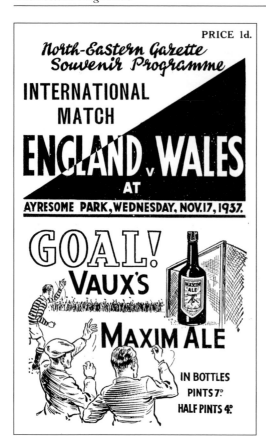

England versus Wales at Ayresome Park in 1937.

Football Association rated not only pen pictures, but also photographs. There were advertisements for nine local cinemas, a half-day excursion to London and the Cunard White Star Line's Easter overseas round trips. Surprisingly, the music programme was not to be provided by a band, but by gramaphone records. This programme is, however, most noteworthy for the fact that the game provided a first cap for the great Peter Doherty, then of Blackpool.

Middlesbrough hosted the November 1937 Home International between England and Wales. The *North-Eastern Gazette* souvenir programme cost one old penny and was 9in x 5.5in with plenty of red colour on both covers, including a brewery advertisement on the front. There was an effusive 'Welcome to Tees-side' by the home club's chairman, and three pages of details of the administrators of both countries, as well as a page of detailed and interesting pen pictures for each of the two teams, who were taking part in the first international to be played at Ayresome Park for over twenty-three years.

Among the fourteen pages, there were thirteen advertisements, including three which are full-page – Ross's Weather Proofs (raincoats), Stanton's (football boots) and Hodgson & Downs Ltd (wine merchants).

Research into the football history surrounding this fixture would reveal that Wales, having won the International Championship in the previous season, had two successive wins against England behind them, but on this occasion England won 2-1 with goals by Matthews and Hall. The Welsh goal was scored by Edwin Perry, who had had an unlikely route to international honours – one game for Merthyr Town before a transfer to Bournemouth, then to Thames, Fulham and finally Doncaster Rovers – will the lattermost club ever again field a current full international?

England and Scotland squeezed in an extra international in August 1946, when they met at Maine Road, Manchester, to boost the Bolton Disaster Fund. Manchester City issued an eight-page A5 programme, printed entirely in blue on white paper, with the familiar OXO advertisement on the front page. John Graydon of the *Sporting Chronicle* introduced the match over pages two and three; there was half a page of Maine Road gossip opposite the team selections and the last two internal pages had pen pictures of both squads. The back page carried a full-page advert for Belle Vue, advertising forthcoming speedway, wrestling, rugby and a firework display.

One of the most difficult post-war England home internationals to obtain is the sixteen-page, black-on-white paper programme issued by Huddersfield Town for the game against Holland at Leeds Road on 27 November 1946. One can only speculate as to how many copies were produced in the first place, but the quality of the non-gloss paper is very poor indeed, and few could have survived the ensuing half-century intact. The

England and Scotland met at Maine Road in aid of the Bolton Disaster Fund in August 1946.

programme is in the normal format of Town issues of the time, with advertising predominant and the features short on text. Page three opens with 'Town Spotlight' by the editor, which incorporates pen pictures of the Dutch team. There is a very brief half page on the England team, with pictures restricted to besuited office bearers of the FA. There is a Division One League table, Huddersfield first and reserve team results and fixtures, five quiz questions and answers and a full-page (inside back page) picture of Huddersfield players taking the field. England won the match 8-2, with Tommy Lawton scoring four goals, in front of 33,000 spectators.

Another of the hardest England post-war home programmes to obtain is the game played at Goodison Park against Portugal on 19 May 1951. This is under the 'Festival of Britain' banner, the logo of which appears in red and blue surrounded by the blue background of the cover. One can only speculate as to the climatic conditions that Saturday afternoon, as it appears that very few copies have survived in good condition. What does not help is the easily-marked print finish of the front cover. The programme is A5 in size, was priced at 6d and had twelve white gloss pages with black print. Page two has welcomes from the chairman of the FA and Everton and page three a welcome from the Earl of Athlone. England team group and pen pictures were next, then the teams on the centre page followed by Portuguese team group and pen pictures. The last two pages had a substantial article welcoming the visitors, along with details of buses after the match.

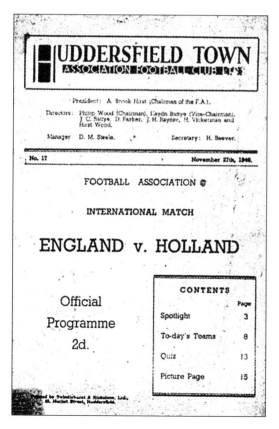

England versus Holland at Huddersfield, 1946.

England versus Portugal at Goodison Park, May 1951.

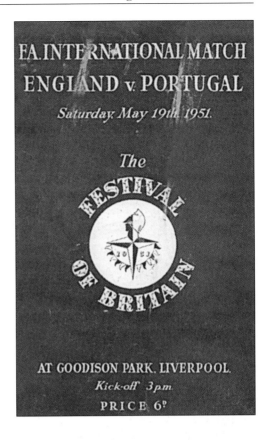

The back page was plain blue, with the 'Festival of Britain' logo in blue and red. Containing absolutely no advertisements, this is a good programme for its time.

Arsenal issued an untypically colourful programme for the England *v.* Sweden match played at Highbury on 19 November 1947. There were only eight pages, A5 in size and similar in typography to post-war Arsenal programmes, but the colour scheme of dark blue and deep yellow owed more to the Swedish colours than to the traditional hue of London N5. Page two had a welcome in both languages, opposite six head and shoulders photographs of the office bearers of both associations. The centre spread had teams on one page and one or two paragraphs on the fixture opposite. There were two pages of pen pictures, with head and shoulder photographs of George Hardwick and H. Nilsson. On the back page were England results since the war, First Division tables of both countries, with the English clubs represented in the match highlighted, a note of Notts County's position in Division Three (South), as Tommy Lawton played for them, and a note of the next two matches to be played at Highbury. The English team line-up had Matthews, Mortensen, Lawton, Mannion and Finney in attack, but Sweden had Gren, Nordahl and Leidholm as inside forwards.

Sunderland invariably issued programmes with large pages for the series of representative matches they hosted at Roker Park in the 1950s – despite their own programmes being consistently smaller. For the visit of Wales on Home International

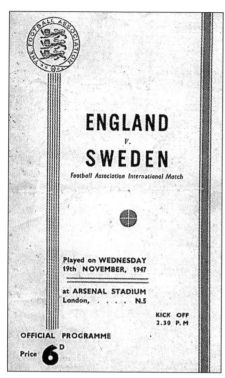

Left: *England versus Sweden at Highbury, November 1947.* Right: *England versus Wales at Sunderland, November 1950.*

business on Wednesday 15 November 1950, a large sixteen-page issue was produced, with the cover printed in black, red and white. The remainder of the programme was printed black on white gloss. Page two was completely blank, opposite the team lines on page three. There was a welcome from the Sunderland chairman and 'Some Historical Facts' on the Football Association on page five, continued on pages six and seven, finishing with a photograph of Sir Stanley Rous (then secretary of the FA). The centre pages had a list of results from the fixture going back to 1879, and the start of England pen pictures and head and shoulder photographs of players. These filled the next two pages, and then it was the turn of the Welsh team for three pages before the inside back page was left completely blank – as was the back page, save for the name of the printers. Rarely had so much space been wasted in a big match programme.

Like England, Scotland also played international matches at grounds other than the national stadium (Hampden Park) in the decades preceding the Second World War. Anticipating smaller crowds for some matches, they were taken to grounds of limited capacity. Consequently, fewer programmes were printed and they are therefore now even rarer than pre-war Hampden programmes (which are hard enough to obtain).

To modern eyes, Firhill, Partick Thistle's ground, would be an unlikely setting for a full international, but it hosted the Scotland *v.* Ireland match in February 1929. Pen pictures of the Scottish team were included in the twenty-page, 3d issue, as well as a page on the caps won by the players of both sides. The only photographs were of SFA officials, a feature of pre-war programmes for all countries – presumably the president, secretary and treasurer of the respective Football Associations were considered to be more important than the players! Also included is a list of the results of the games between the two countries dating back to Scotland's 5-0 win in 1884. Ireland won this game by the only goal. Needless to say, such a programme would only now be sold at auction, for several hundred pounds.

Two years later, Celtic Park was the venue for Ireland's next visit to Glasgow. Another twenty-page programme, with a more attractive blue cover, was produced for the occasion. This time pen pictures of both teams were included as were head and shoulders photographs of both teams, making the programme a much better-looking issue. Not to be outdone there were also photographs of the Scottish and Irish officials, a facts and figures page and the list of previous results. Scotland won the game 3-1.

Eighteen months later saw the 1931/32 Scotland v. Ireland game played earlier in the season. Ibrox was the venue for the September clash. A similiar programme to that produced for the Celtic Park clash was issued, although the price was reduced to 2d. Again pen pictures and photographs of each player were included. One of the more interesting

Scotland versus Ireland at Partick Thistle's Firhill Park in 1928.

Scottish Football Association Ltd.

Official Programme

International

SCOTLAND

versus

IRELAND

TYNECASTLE PARK
Edinburgh

Wednesday, 13th November
1935

Kick-off - 2-30 p.m.

N. Adshead & Son, Printers, 34 Cadogan Street
and 11 Union Street, Glasgow.

Scotland versus Ireland at Hearts' Tynecastle Park in 1935.

advertisements included Thomson's bus service, on which you could travel from Glasgow to London for 30 shillings single or 50 shillings return. Ireland were captained by Jimmy Dunne, who seemed to be the only southerner in the side.

Ireland's next visit to Glasgow was in 1933 and the game was played at Celtic Park. The programme for this fixture was similar to that of previous issues with a pale blue cover, however this time the SFA badge featured. This was another twenty-page programme which again included photographs of the players and officials but was not priced; the programme of music also got a page. Ireland won the game 2-1 in a side that included Dublin-born Alec Stevenson of Rangers. Stevenson is actually the only player to have played for Rangers and what is now the Republic of Ireland. Although he was never capped for the Republic during his Rangers career, he was good enough for an all-Ireland team under the auspices of the Irish Football Association (Northern Ireland). It does actually appear that players were only considered for one team during this period as the other southern player on the Ireland side, J. McMahon of Bohemians, was never capped for the south. Very little is written regarding the relationships between the two associations at this time, but they appear to have been difficult.

Two years later, Ireland got to visit Edinburgh as Tynecastle was the venue for the latest instalment of the Scotland *v.* Ireland fixture. This time the programme only contained sixteen pages and was not priced. This is still a very attractive item, with the photographs the most striking feature. A page was included on international records. Again none of the three Southern-born players (Alec Stevenson, Harry Duggan or Jimmy Kelly) were capped by the South. Scotland won the game 2-1.

Pittodrie Stadium, Aberdeen, was the venue for the 1937 game between the two countries. A twenty-four page dark blue programme was produced, costing 3d. This is another excellent issue with lots of great photographs, including interesting reading material on the British championship and various soccer items. Yet again it is fascinating to note that Tommy Breen of Man Utd made the side but failed to appear in the South's two World Cup qualifiers against Norway during the same period. This is the best of the programmes for this fixture and probably also the one which turns up most often on offers lists. The six programmes of the series described above were quite similar yet attractive issues.

The turning point for English international football – and for the game in general on the British Isles – was England's first defeat at the hands of a Continental country. It was not so much that milestone, as the manner of it – beaten 6-3 by a Hungarian team that was superior in every department at Wembley on 25 November 1953. For the game, which proved to be so significant, Wembley Stadium issued their familiar smallish-sized,

A notable date in English football history – the visit of the Hungarians to Wembley in 1953.

twenty-page programme, printed in black ink on white semi-gloss paper with red, green and blue colour on the cover pages. As was the tradition, the flags of the competing countries (albeit the Union Jack that was used for England) and the Association Crests accompanied the aerial photograph of a packed Wembley, in blue, on the front cover. It was priced at the conventional 1/-. Contents included the programme of arrangements and music, a welcome in two languages, a page of narrative on the visitors, pen pictures of both teams, photographs of the last England home match, an eerily appropriate full-page article entitled 'Soccer Pupils and the Old Professor', a couple of photographs of Hungary and past and present fixture details. The advertisers were as predictable as the format and contents – *Radio Times*, Wembley events, Taylor Walker's Special Pale Ale and Bovril.

Despite supplies being relatively plentiful for Wembley internationals, the England *v.* Hungary programme sells for around £20, largely because of its significance and collectability – some three times more than the 1953 England *v.* Scotland programme, for instance. Most major dealers have sufficient supplies to include the programme on their sales catalogue, without the need to entertain offers.

Despite the growing recognition of the need to learn from foreign football powers, the big set-piece internationals of each season were the England *v.* Scotland matches which climaxed the British Home International Championship. In 1961, England thrashed Scotland 9-3 at Wembley. The stadium issued their familiar programme for the latest clash of the Auld Enemy, with an aerial photograph of the stadium in blue and background design in blue, red and green on the front cover. As programmes of its time went, this was a reasonable issue, albeit the cover price of 1/- being double the price of most ordinary League programmes. The sixteen pages included articles on the forthcoming World Cup finals and the future of Scottish football, as well as detailed pen pictures of both squads and action photographs of the previous year's meeting at Hampden. There were portraits of the guests of honour, the Queen and the Duke of Edinburgh, and opposite the centre page and the team line-ups (in 2-3-5 formation) was the familiar timetable and programme of music. Advertisements included the *Radio Times* (on the inside front page), Bovril, featuring Jimmy Greaves in a Chelsea strip (on the back page), Double Diamond beers (inside back page), British European Airways, Senior Service cigarettes and forthcoming ice hockey, greyhound racing and football events at the stadium.

The programme is very commonplace and should not cost much more than £2 to buy from one of the major dealers, who will certainly have several copies in stock. The irony of the programme is that for the match dubbed 'Haffey's Wembley', after the hapless Celtic and Scotland goalkeeper, the listed netminder was Laurie Leslie of Airdrie, who withdrew through injury.

Perversely, that result heralded a sequence of better results for Scotland against the Auld Enemy, culminating in their 3-2 victory at Wembley in 1967 – England's first defeat since winning the World Cup. By the mid-1960s Wembley programmes were more changeable and more colourful after two decades of the same format. Nonetheless, 1/- still bought only sixteen standard-sized (A5) pages, headed by an aerial photograph of the stadium with spot colour of green, blue and red for decoration **(8)**. Brian Glanville of the *Sunday Times* wrote the page three article headed 'England Roar Today?' and Gair Henderson of the *Glasgow Evening Times* declared in the page eleven article that it was

'Haffey's Wembley', the 9-3 drubbing suffered by Scotland in 1961.

'Scots' Pride at Stake!'. Jack Rollin compiled a page of match facts and there were two action shots of the 1965 match. Detailed pen pictures of both squads filled a page each, and the timetable and programme of music was, as always at this time, present. Team selections were spread over both centre pages. Even the adverts were familiar – *Radio Times*, Double Diamond, Bovril on the back page, and Cadets and Players No. 6 cigarettes. Elsewhere in London, West Ham, Chelsea and, to a lesser extent Spurs and Arsenal, were developing modern, informative programmes which showed this big match issue to be rather dated and overpriced. In common with most England home Wembley programmes of the 1960s, this is by no means a rare issue, although interest in Scotland has recently edged the price up to around £5.

It is now appropriate to pause in our narrative of the development (or, in some cases, the regression) of the match programme, and consider some practical tips about how to obtain football programmes and, just as importantly, how to maintain a collection. Having (possibly) spent substantial sums of money obtaining older items – in effect pieces of frail, folded paper – it makes some sense to look after them and attempt to halt any natural deterioration in their condition.

Collecting Tips: Looking after your collection

After a few months, or maybe a season's accumulation, the pile of programmes that constitutes an early collection will begin to topple over and become scattered over the bedroom floor. Setting up a method of storing programmes is an important intermediate step in a programme collection. Storing flat is not recommended as programmes come in all shapes and sizes and stacking them one on top of another will cause corners to curl. It is much better to store them upright, but adequately supported to ensure that they are completely vertical and not curling at the bottom (standing) edge. A shoe box is the traditional method of storing programmes initially, although that was when they were A5 (small) in size and before today's brochure-sized Wembley and big match issues. A larger style of box, of strong cardboard, such as a whisky or wine carton, is ideal, having the additional benefit of being fully enclosed with top flap, thereby keeping out the sunlight which discolours paper over a period of time.

There are basic rules for looking after programmes – keep them free of creases, folds and any writing, marks or blemishes. Keep them out of direct sunlight and in a dry, well-ventilated environment. Damp conditions will lead to rusting staples and mould forming on the pages, giving an unpleasant 'musty' smell. Too much sunlight and lack of ventilation will lead to paper yellowing and becoming brittle and flaking. Cellars are not recommended, attics are not ideal – in fact it is not too fanciful to recommend that a programme collections' living conditions should match those of its owner. At the match, take a plastic bag to keep the programme dry and free of folds and creases and don't write team selections or half-time scores on the pages.

Collecting Tips: Really looking after your collection

While a programme records the contemporary circumstances in which a match is played, it is understandable for collectors to wish to record details of the 90 minutes which the programme will come to represent. There is a strong temptation to record team changes, scorers and result on the face of the programme, particularly on the team line-up page. This should be avoided as markings on programmes greatly diminish their value and attractiveness in later years. The preferred system is to enclose a newspaper cutting of a match report within the pages of the programme (do not use sellotape or staples). This is a particularly satisfactory method if programmes are stored in individual bags or envelopes. There are many methods of storing programmes – each depending on the resources available to the collector. For rare or old programmes, or those of particular value to the collector, insertion in plastic folders or sleeves in a ring binder is the preferred method. For all other programmes in a collection, it is worth investing in a large quantity of polypropylene bags, into which programmes may be inserted. The unused area of the bags can then be folded over for added protection. Enclosed in these polypropylene bags, the programmes are afforded a high degree of protection from creasing, marking, discolouring and any other kind of damage which may befall fragile pieces of paper. The bags are also transparent, thus allowing instant identification, which is not allowed by other popular methods of storage, such as paper bags or envelopes. Any of these storage devices would need to be obtained, in the quantities for a sizeable or growing collection, from a specialist stockist or manufacturer. Once in bags or envelopes, programmes can then be filed in box files, whisky or wine cartons, wallet files and other methods of storage which best suit collecting specialities. The twenty-five or so programmes which constitute a home season's issues, for instance, can be stored in one standard wallet file. Several seasons' international match programmes can be placed in a box file, while around thirty post-war Cup Final programmes can also be stored in such a file. Painstakingly accumulated, carefully stored, programmes of a quantity in excess of, say, 500, will require to be catalogued for easy reference, a subject we shall explore later in the book.

World Cup finals

Football matches don't come any bigger than World Cup finals, and there is a growing interest in collecting all memorabilia surrounding World Cup tournaments. Items from the three pre-war finals and the 1950 tournament in Brazil are extremely rare and attract massive bids when they appear, infrequently, at auction.

The very rare tournament programme for the 1934 World Cup finals in Italy cost one collector over £6,000 at auction, while the match programme for the 1938 World Cup final, between Hungary and Italy in Paris, was sold for £6,700. This was an eight-page programme, which measured 8.5in x 10.5in and included caricatures and profiles of the two teams, details of previous World Cups and the results of the 1938 World Cup finals.

The vary rare tournament brochure from the 1950 World Cup finals in Brazil.

The centre page spread featured local adverts and the layout of the two teams and officials. The cover price of the programme (2 francs) was expensive for its time, when contemporary British programmes were selling for 6d, and the rarity of the item was illustrated in the price it achieved at auction – the auctioneers were expecting a top bid of around £2,000. The tournament programme for the 1938 Finals cost a buyer more than £4,300 at auction.

The first World Cup tournament to have widely available programmes was held in Switzerland in 1954. Individual programmes were issued for all the games and they can be obtained for upwards of £20 from leading dealers' catalogues. They resembled British programmes in page size (A5) but each comprised thirty-six pages – at least twice the size of contemporary British issues. The only colour was on the cover sheet; the front page and three other advertising pages had scarlet and light blue along with black and white. The internal thirty-two pages were black on poor quality white paper. After a welcome in four languages, there was coverage in words and pictures of the two teams, centre fold team selections, and then a second half giving details of the tournament, previous World Cup finals and photographs of the Swiss stadia. At least 50 per cent of the pages were advertisements. The programme for the final, between West Germany and Hungary, attracts offers in excess of £100.

Following on the example shown by the 1954 finals in Switzerland, programmes were issued for every game played four years later in Sweden. These were small in size, being slimmer and shorter than the conventional A5 issues of the time, but with plenty of pages, and had identical covers until the final match. The programmes prior to the final had a four-colour design on a basically black background, but this design was abandoned – and lightened – for the Sweden *v.* Brazil match. The ninety-two pages contained many features, photographs of stadia, statistics and copious advertising, and represented a substantial souvenir of a major occasion.

The 1958 finals, with all four British home countries competing, were widely covered in the UK and programmes were relatively plentiful in this country in the years that followed. As the decades have passed, they have become much rarer; the more plentiful games sell for around £15 each, while the programme for the final sells for no less than £50 and sometimes up to double that amount **(9)**.

In common with South American practice, the tournament programme for the 1962 finals held in Chile is extremely rare and expensive, and for the 1970 finals in Mexico, a multilingual brochure was published in England by *Queen* magazine, under licence from FIFA and the Mexican FA, and is accepted as the official programme of the tournament. However, it was printed in such quantities that so many remain readily available that they can be obtained for little more than £1. Cover price was 6/- and, with decimalisation looming, underneath was '30p'.

The type style and page layout of the sixty-eight page brochure signalled a revolution in programme design and the contents were attractively presented in four (colour coded) languages. There were two pages of welcome, a three-page history of the competition, two pages on the qualifying tournament, a page on each of the competing nations listing their squads (with head and shoulder photographs of some of the players, arranged in group order) and a preceding page on the venues. There were eight pages in which results and

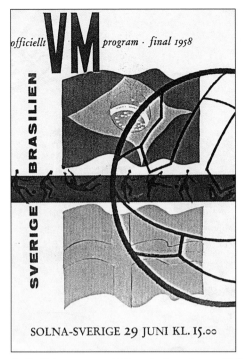

Left: *Pele announced his arrival on the world football scene in the 1958 World Cup final, Sweden versus Brazil.* Right: *Another rare World Cup finals programme from South America – Chile in 1962.*

team selections could be entered for the matches. The front cover had the image of the Jules Rimet Trophy – which, as it transpired, was in its final competition – in yellow and blue on a red background.

There were no individual programmes for the 1966 World Cup finals held in England. Instead, the tournament brochure was available widely before and during the tournament, and on sale at every match up to the final. This was a seventy-two page brochure, with the Jules Rimet Trophy in gold superimposed on a graphic of the world and England in blue, green and white. The tournament logo was in colour in the top left-hand corner **(10)**.

There were full page photographs of the Queen and Earl of Harewood (patron and president of the FA) and a welcome from the late J.H.W. Mears and Sir Stanley Rous in four languages. There were four pages in words and pictures on the organising committee, a map of the venues, a programme of the opening ceremony, two pages of results from the qualifying competition, the colours of the finalists and a page on each finalist, with head and shoulders photographs surrounding the squad list. Eleven pages were set aside for the fixtures, with space to complete team selections, results, scorers and so on, and two blank pages were provided for notes. There was a fairly heavy advertising presence and the only full-colour advert, on the back page, was for Cadets Cigarettes. The programmes were produced in massive quantities and are not at all scarce. Expect to pay no more than £2 for a copy.

For the final, between England and West Germany, the only single-match issue of the tournament was in the same style, size and format as the tournament brochure, but the full colour illustration was of the Jules Rimet Trophy and the tournament logo on a blue background. The bulk of the sixty-eight pages consisted of results and action photographs of the matches in the finals. Squad details of all sixteen countries and the qualifying tournament results were copied from the tournament brochure. There were messages of welcome in four languages from various officials, four pages listing FIFA delegates (with photographs), and full-page portraits of the the the Queen and the Earl of Harewood.

Apart from the welcomes and the photograph captions, the only text of note was a one-page history of the World Cup, and while this substantial brochure is a fitting souvenir of the occasion, the matchday buyer did not received a great deal of entertainment for his 2/6d. The centre fold has head and shoulders photographs of the twenty-two players in both squads and a space for writing in the chosen twenty-two and the result. Many original purchasers did just that, with the result that unmarked copies now sell at a premium.

Until recently, the programme was available for £5, but the price has increased quite steeply in recent months, and you may have to pay up to £15. Most major dealers have sufficient stocks to include it on their sales catalogues. Unfortunately, the programme was illegally reproduced a number of years after the match, and while experienced collectors and dealers discriminate between the two programmes, many newer collectors unsuspectingly have a reproduction in their collection.

In 1974, the Germans issued a substantial, pocket-slim style of tournament brochure, with a separate updating booklet with squad details. This is becoming rarer with the passing years and now sells for around £10. Keeping with their normal practice, many of the host clubs issued 'stadium edition' programmes for individual games, in the style of their normal match programmes. These may be regarded as official programmes and sell for between £15 and £20 **(11)**.

The most comprehensive World Cup finals programme to date was published by the organisers of the 1978 finals in Argentina and was a slim, perfectly-bound volume of over 300 pages with a grey laminated cover, on which was text in black print and the tournament logo in light blue, white and black. There were no programmes for individual games and the tournament programme was widely available throughout the country and at matches.

Contents were entirely in Spanish, starting with a twenty-page history of the World Cup, then sixty pages on the location of the matches. The competing nations were each given four pages and then there was a series of half-page team groups. The comprehensive brochure finished with a number of features on numismatics, philately, officials' uniforms, official passes, stadium maps, television and a page for each fixture with space to complete match details. Blank pages were provided for notes and autographs. The majority of the pages were in black and white, but a number featured full colour.

Closer to the tournament, a thirty-two page black and white booklet, slightly smaller in size, was published as an insert and this included the final squad lists for the competing countries. The programme was produced in huge quantities and brought into the UK in good numbers, so copies may be purchased for £1.50.

The tournament brochure for the 1978 World Cup finals in Argentina.

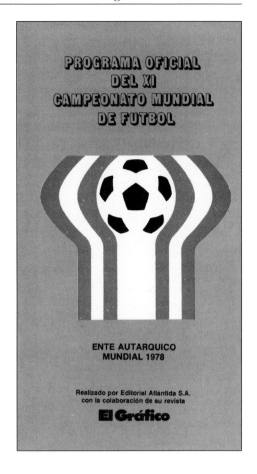

A British-produced programme was the official production for the 1982 finals in Spain, although there were a handful of 'stadium editions', notably for Scotland's group matches in Malaga. This glossy, colourful brochure **(12)** almost certainly owed its production to the San Miguel beer company! The tournament programme for 1986 in Mexico is harder to obtain and costs in excess of £25, while individual match programmes for some of the games in Italy in 1990 may be obtained for little more than £5. Various programmes were issued for the 1994 finals in USA and they can be purchased for around £7, while the tournament brochure for 1998 in France is readily available and costs £5.

Four
At Home

Club issues

By far the most popular of collecting categories is that which concentrates on a favourite club. At its most basic, this can encompass home first team programmes only. Away match programmes may be added, as could those from reserve and youth team games (home and/or away) and friendly matches. You could collect current issues only, or go back to a particular time period. Each level has its own costs and degree of difficulty in obtaining issues. Generally, 90 per cent of all programmes issued over the past twenty-five years may be obtained with little difficulty, at cover prices, from club shops, programme fairs and dealers' catalogues. Reserve and youth team programmes are much more obscure, due to their low print runs and disposable nature. Programmes from friendly or cup matches played abroad may prove in some instances to be difficult to obtain, and there will inevitably be the odd domestic League or cup match which had a particularly low print run (compared with attendance) which will result in a much sought-after programme. Those for the early 1970s may be fairly readily available from dealers' catalogues, particularly from local traders who are more likely to carry larger stocks of local clubs, at prices around 50p or the cover price. Late 1940s League programmes could cost between £5 and £10 to buy, whilst 1950s programmes range from up to £5 for 1950/51, down to £1.50 for 1959/60. Programmes from the 1960s cost between £1.50 and 75p although an increasing number of these are appearing on 'offers lists' as opposed to straight sales catalogues.

Programmes from around 1955 and before can fall into one of two categories – more expensive to buy at around £2, or much sought after and the subject of offers only. It is harder to evaluate the price of programmes which find themselves onto dealers' offers lists, particularly those involving popular clubs whose programmes are generally in demand. However, the minimum offer quoted by the dealer is often a reasonable guide to the level at which bidding should start. Generally, a bid around the normal list price will secure most items – but a collector requiring a particular programme may have to bid high to complete a set. Pre-war and wartime, and those for the reconstruction seasons immediately after the Second World War, are invariably subject to offers and some of them can be very expensive indeed.

Home is where the heart is

Collecting home match programmes of a favourite club is a bit of a daunting prospect, given the numbers involved (up to twenty programmes per season since 1960, for example, amounts to some 800 different issues) and the lack of variety of style and design within a season's programmes may not make this the most interesting option available. On the other hand, season ticket holders and regular spectators will have a headstart to their collection by simply hanging on to the programme they buy every other week, and the end product of a large 'homes' collection is a thorough record of the comings and goings, ups and downs, triumphs and disasters, at the club over the chosen period. The club shop or local dealer will readily supply those items missed along the way and either source, as well as the larger catalogue-issuing national dealers, could help put together a fairly comprehensive collection of programmes back to 1970 without too much trouble and at reasonable cost. The flexibility of programme collecting to fit the pockets and ambitions of collectors is shown to its full advantage here, as a collection of home League match programmes from 1970 is readily obtainable and would comprise upwards of 600 issues, which alone constitutes a decent collection – and one that would be added to as each new season unfolds.

There are occasional 'rare' issues amongst the hundreds of normal League programmes – a hiccup at the printers, an unusually large attendance, particularly inclement weather on the day of the match – all these factors, and a few more exotic reasons, can reduce the supply of available programmes. Demand can also affect availability and hence price – the visit of a 'collectable' club (such as Manchester United, Liverpool, Leeds United, Spurs or Arsenal) inspires more interest in that programme, while clubs who are currently enjoying a period of popularity after years in the dodrums (Newcastle, Sunderland and Middlesbrough spring immediately to mind) cause an upsurge in interest in their older programmes with a new found army of collectors eager to make up for lost time.

Circumstances – usually tragic – often propel ordinary League programmes into much sought-after programmes. None of the huge crowd at Highbury for the visit of Manchester United in February 1958 would have suspected that this was to be the last game on British soil for the 'Busby Babes', many of whom would perish at Munich airport within the week.

The programme brought out for the match was prepared and presented as any other Arsenal home issue for the 1957/58 season. Sixteen A5 pages, it was ahead of its time in content, size and design and was excellent value at 6d. The 'Voice of Arsenal' fills the first three internal pages, much of which are given over to the visitors, and page five has a full match report of Arsenal's previous fixture. There are two pages of match action photographs and then the centre fold team line-ups, followed by United pen pictures. 'Jottings by Spectator' devotes two pages (less the space used for the half-time scoreboard) to notes from the history of United, followed by a full-page team group shot of the visitors. Two pages of statistics and a full page 'Portrait Gallery' of Vic Groves brings the programme to its conclusion, where forthcoming matches and previous match details cover the back page. The content is packed in with a small type size and an absence of advertisements. Arsenal programmes of this vintage are extremely commonplace, but the historical significance of this game means that it fetches upwards of £25 under offer.

Manchester United *v.* Sheffield Wednesday in the FA Cup would have been an unremarkable fixture with a routine programme, but in 1958 this was United's first home match after the Munich tragedy. The programme is renowned for two aspects: the front page message from the club chairman and the blank spaces on the United line-up in the centre pages. The entire programme is devoted to the tragedy: page two is a tribute to the United secretary, Walter Crickmer; page three to trainers Tom Curry and Bert Whalley; pages four and five to the seven players (at that date) who had died. In the

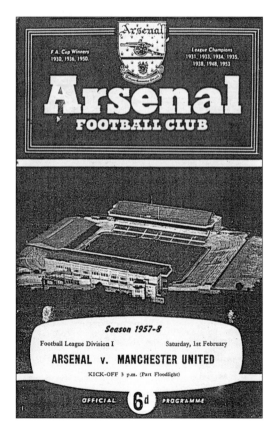

The Busby Babes' last match on British soil at Highbury on 1 February 1958.

Perhaps the most poignant of all programmes – Manchester United were unable to predict their starting eleven in the immediate aftermath of Munich and so eleven spaces were left blank in the centre pages.

second half of the programme, there was a page on the injured who remained in Munich, opposite pen pictures of Sheffield Wednesday. The inside back pages were devoted to the journalists who perished, including two contributors to the *United Review*, Alf Clarke and Tom Jackson. The back page gave details of memorial services. The only adverts in the 4d programme surrounded the centre page team sheet.

Home League programmes represent the most obvious and most convenient collecting set, and will allow the purchase of programmes at a greater rate and number than other categories, but it is for the collector with stamina and staying power and, depending on the start date chosen, deep pocket.

Playing away

Many collectors restrict their collection to home match programmes, reasoning that this reflects their football attending habits, and the programmes are, after all, the product of their favourite club. The majority of club collectors, however, widen their collection to include away matches.

Collectors may be fortunate in travelling with their favourite team on a regular basis and they can purchase the programmes for themselves. Alternatively, they may have friends or relatives who can do this for them. On the other hand, they may be reliant on the club souvenir shop or supporters programme stall for the opportunity to purchase the issue for the previous week's away game. In the rustic days of pre-commercialised football, there was a convention of a quantity of programmes being brought back by the visiting team in the kit hamper, for sale at their ground the following week. That happened on a reciprocal basis, thus guaranteeing supply for non-travelling fans. One suspects that this forms no more part of the modern game than the wicker hamper that once transported them. Supply now falls to the initiative of the club shop manager or keen supporters officials and is very much a matter of close scrutiny and market justification, given the high print cost and cover price of current season programmes.

The keenest of collectors entrust their supply line to the Royal Mail and faithfully write to the home club prior to each of their club's away fixtures. If this is done in time to ensure the arrival of the letter by the day before the match, then supply is virtually guaranteed, irrespective of whether the match programme is a 'sell out'. The programme will usually arrive within a day or two of the fixture, although some clubs are still notoriously tardy in replying. There are two major drawbacks to this apparently ideal arrangement. The first and most obvious is the additional cost of postage both ways. The majority of League club programmes are heavier than 60g and will therefore require return postage of 41p (33p second class) or even 72p (54p second), in addition to the 27p or 19p to post the request. If payment is made by postal order the poundage is a further cost – it is best to pay by cheque (left blank and endorsed 'not to exceed £…' if the cover price is unknown). The other less obvious consideration is the condition of the programme once it has been through the post. Although clubs invariably use good quality envelopes, they can be subject to some rough handling and the programmes may have a crease or two when they arrive.

Aside from mailing or other costs, away match programme collecting need be neither more nor less expensive that home issue collecting, with the laws of supply and demand for popular fixtures and collectable clubs applying in equal measure. For those who concentrate exclusively on home issues, an extension into away match issues will prove to be varied and rewarding – and that little bit more intriguing in terms of tracking down past programmes, as well as those of the current season. By the inter-war years, every English League club was issuing a matchday programme and a handful in Scotland followed suit, as did most of the senior non-League clubs south of the border. The existence of these pre-war programmes is something of a 'tease' for collectors because they are very rare and therefore very expensive. The majority of collectors content themselves with a handful, or even one, of these items, and restrict the bulk of their collection to rather less expensive and more obtainable recent issues. Most concentrate on their favourite club.

Top club programmes through the Depression

The dreadful, debilitating economic depression of the 1930s had little impact on the style and standard of football programmes. Clubs continued to produce fairly

Left: *Sunderland's black cat shares the front cover of 1930s programmes with an advert for the local ale.* Right: *What the well-dressed Geordie was wearing – according to this Newcastle programme from 1936/37.*

substantial 1d or 2d issues and they appeared to include as many advertisements as before, suggesting that programme revenue did not suffer the same fate as the rest of the economy. In terms of the quality and quantity of issues, the advances of the previous decade were consolidated and programmes changed little between 1930 and 1939.

Pre-war programmes from the North-East of England are notoriously difficult to obtain today, but Sunderland's 1930s programmes were substantial twelve-page productions with a splash of red ink on the front cover of an otherwise black-and-white issue. In common with most clubs at the time, there were no match details on the cover, simply the name of the club and a crest or logo, although the major part of the front page was devoted to an advertisement. These, presumably expensive, adverts were invariably for well-known local industries or enterprises. In Sunderland's case it was for Vaux Beers.

Newcastle United also issued an excellent pre-war programme, comprising sixteen pages, printed dark grey on white paper. A sketch of two footballers shared club details at the top of the cover, which was dominated by an advert for the *Sunday Sun* newspaper. In 1936/37, the format was changed to a larger page size and the masthead featured only one player, kicking a football with the programme price (1d) superimposed; the dominant advertisement was for a gentlemens' outfitters.

The Sheffield clubs issued handsome programmes of contrasting styles. Wednesday abandoned their long-standing small size with team lines on the front, to produce a splendid large-page edition with a striking sketch of Hillsborough's main stand on the front cover. The half-page advertisement was for a local product – razor blades. Sheffield United favoured a smaller size, in sixteen pages, with red and white stripes on the cover and an aerial sketch of Bramall Lane showing the old cricket pitch and pavilion.

Fairly brief programmes were preferred by some of the top clubs – West Ham and Tottenham shared a similar style, with a very large folded sheet. There were few, if any, advertisements and the type size was very small with plenty of reading crammed in. The price was an undemanding 1d, although it is surprising to see such prominent clubs issue such brief programmes. Chelsea were scarely better – although they put their name to an eight-page production. Amongst the teams in the capital, it was Arsenal who produced by far the most impressive pre-war programme, with a sixteen-page edition sporting a deep red card cover advertising Highbury's enviable local transport links.

Blackburn's 1935/36 programme cover could have come from an earlier decade – or century – with a very old fashioned mast-head, and the gentleman in the outfitter's sketch dressed in a wing collar.

Left: *Sheffield Wednesday feature their stadium and local produce on the front of their 1936/37 programme.* Right: *Across the city, United had abandoned the time-honoured front page advertisements in favour of red and white stripes by the time this local derby programme was issued in October 1938.*

(1) *The first ever* Villa News and Record, *dated 1 September 1906.* **(2)** *1981 FA Cup final.*

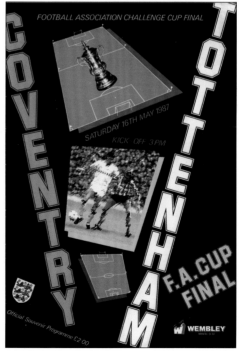

(3) *1981 FA Cup final replay.* **(4)** *1987 FA Cup final.*

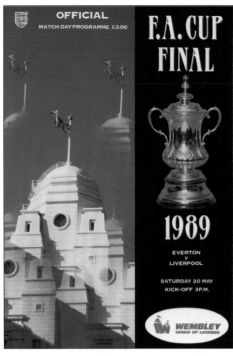

(5) *1989 FA Cup final.* **(6)** *A Birmingham pre-war programme from April 1923.*

(7) *England under-23 versus Scotland under-23 at Middlesbrough, March 1961.* **(8)** *England versus Scotland, 1967.*

(9) *1958 World Cup finals.* **(10)** *1966 World Cup finals brochure.*

(11) *1974 World Cup finals brochure.* **(12)** *A 1982 World Cup programme for group matches played in Malaga.*

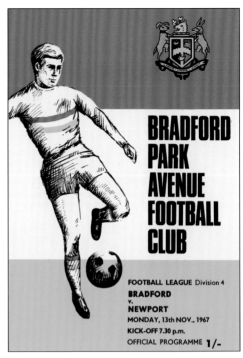

(13) *Newport County, 1973.* **(14)** *Bradford Park Avenue, 1967.*

(15) *RAF versus Scotland, 1944.* **(16)** *Scotland versus England, 1943.*

3.

EMPIRE STADIUM

WEMBLEY

Managing Director - A. J. ELVIN

Saturday FEBRUARY 19th, 1944

Kick-off 3.0 p.m.

ASSOCIATION FOOTBALL MATCH

ENGLAND

v.

SCOTLAND

In aid of WAR CHARITIES

OFFICIAL PROGRAMME SIXPENCE

AIR RAID PRECAUTIONS.

In the event of an Air Raid Alert, if aircraft are reported in the immediate vicinity of the Stadium, spectators will be requested to leave the enclosures and make their way quietly to the Circulating Corridors under the Stands as directed by the Stewards and Officials. Those wishing to leave the Stadium may do so by any of the usual Exits.

(17) *England versus Scotland, 1944.*

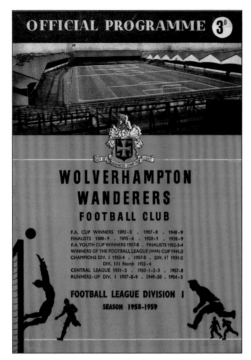

(18) *Wolverhampton Wanderers, 1958/59.* **(19)** *Bradford City, 1959.*

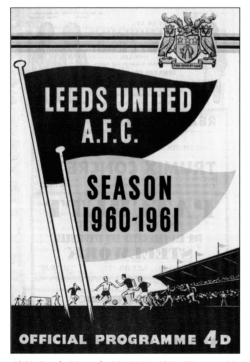

(20) *Leeds United, 1960/61.* **(21)** *Torquay United, 1960.*

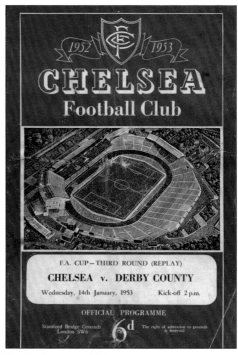

(22) *Oldham Athletic, 1961.* **(23)** *Chelsea versus Derby County, 1953.*

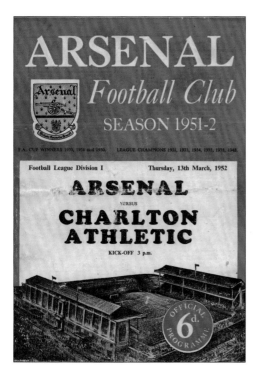

(24) *Arsenal versus Charlton Athletic, 1952.* **(25)** *Tottenham Hotspur versus Athletico Madrid, 1963.*

(**26**) *Real Madrid versus Stade Reims, European Cup final, 1959.* (**27**) *Real Madrid versus Eintracht Frankfurt, ECF, 1960.*

(**28**) *Celtic versus Inter Milan, ECF, 1967.* (**29**) *Manchester United versus Benfica, ECF, 1968.*

(30) *Celtic versus Leeds, 1970 European Cup semi-final.*

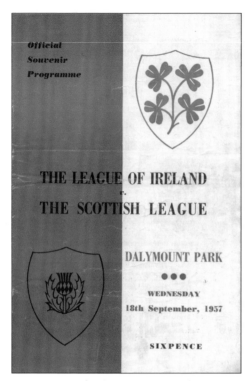

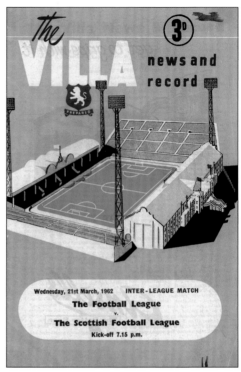

(31) *League of Ireland versus Scottish League, 1957.* **(32)** *English League versus Scottish League, 1962.*

(33) *Torquay United versus Barrow, 1966.* **(34)** *Crystal Palace football programme, October 1960.*

(35) Glentoran Gazette, *1967.* **(36)** *Orgryte versus Malmo, 1973.*

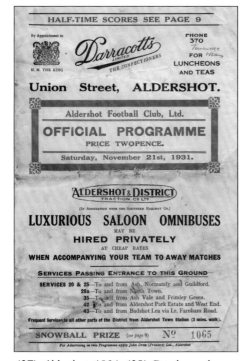

(37) *Aldershot, 1931.* **(38)** *Peterborough versus Corby Town, 1957.*

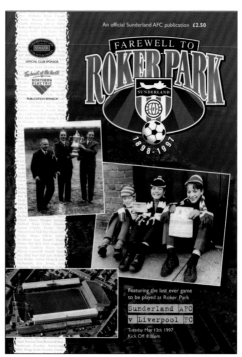

(39) *Cambridge versus Chelsea, 1970.* **(40)** *Last match at Roker Park: Sunderland versus Liverpool, 1997.*

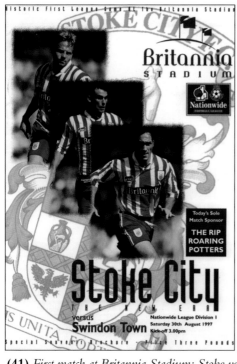

(41) *First match at Britannia Stadium: Stoke versus Swindon, 1997.* **(42)** *Last match at Burnden Park: Bolton versus Charlton, 1997.*

(43) *First match at Reebok Stadium: Bolton versus Everton, 1997*

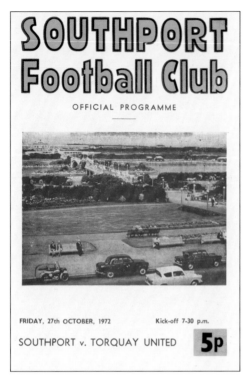

(44) *Southport versus Torquay, 1972.* **(45)** *Wycombe Wanderers versus Oxford City, 1972.*

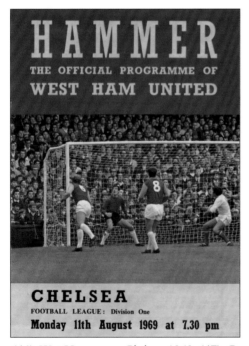

(46) *West Ham versus Chelsea, 1969.* **(47)** *Coventry City versus Arsenal, 1970s.*

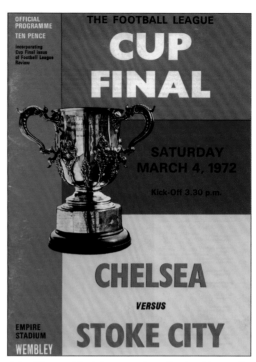

(48) *Queens Park Rangers versus West Bromwich Albion, 1967 League Cup final.* **(49)** *Stoke versus Chelsea, 1972 League Cup final.*

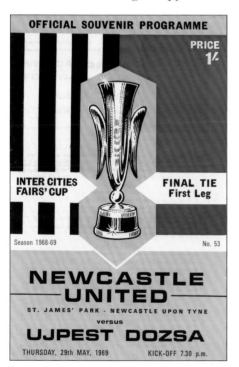

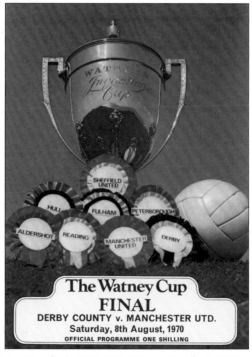

(50) *Newcastle versus Ujpest Dosza, Inter Cities Fairs' Cup final, 1969.* **(51)** *Watney Cup final, 1970.*

(52) *Dryborough Cup final, 1973.* **(53)** *Sir Stan Matthews testimonial, 1965.*

(54) *Bobby Charlton testimonial, 1972.* **(55)** *Jack Charlton testimonial, 1973.*

No concessions to modernity on this
1935/36 Blackburn Rovers programme.

Lower division League club programmes through the Depression

Just as the economic privations of the 1930s had little impact on the style and standard of the top clubs' football programmes, so it also appeared to bypass clubs in the lower divisions of the Football League. They continued to produce fairly substantial 1d or 2d issues, apparently containing as many advertisements as before, again suggesting that programme revenue did not suffer the same fate as the rest of the economy. Indeed, throughout the troubled 1930s, club programmes maintained the advances they had made in the previous decade.

Unlike today, where far larger crowds and considerably greater commercial clout produces a big difference in the standard of programmes issued by England's top clubs compared to those struggling at the bottom of the League, there was little in the quantity and quality of club programmes to suggest their respective status in the game. It was just as likely to find a sixteen-page programme in the Third Division as in the First Division, and vice-versa with eight-page issues, or even the folded sheet programmes – as favoured by West Ham and Tottenham Hotspur at the top level, as well as Mansfield Town further down.

Port Vale, whose pre-war issues are notoriously difficult to obtain today, issued twelve-page programmes with cream and red covers. Southport and New Brighton, both no longer in the League, also ran to twelve pages, as did Darlington – whose pre-war programmes are also

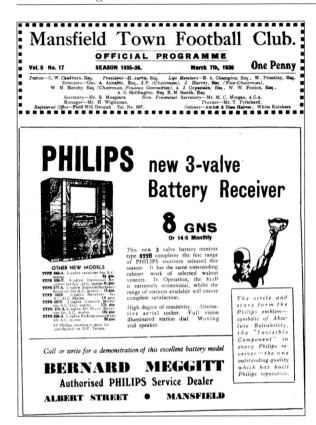

difficult to obtain today. In 1938/39, Bristol City produced as big a programme as had been seen in the country, at thirty-two large pages, with a team group photograph on the pink cover. There were plenty of advertisements, but City managed to include a grid with every result from the Third Division (South) that season. Chester City, in the Third Division (North) in 1934/35, published a large sixteen-page programme for 2d and were one of the few clubs to print precise attendance figures and gate receipts for all their fixtures.

To modern eyes, programmes from former League clubs such as Bradford Park Avenue and Gateshead (eight black and white pages for just 1d in 1937/38) seem from a long-gone era, and none more so than issues from Thames' brief spell in the Third Division (South), for 1930/31 and 1931/32. Their programmes were similar in style to those of West Ham, which was not surprising, given that they shared the Hammers' long-time printers Helliar & Sons of Barking Road, Plaistow. Their 1d programmes consisted of four large pages (one huge folded sheet) with advertisements, the half-time scoreboard and match details on the front, club notes and league tables on page two, team line-ups (in 2-3-5 formation) and adverts on page three, and fixtures, results and more adverts on the back page.

One of the many fascinating features of collecting programmes is tracking the name changes of clubs through the years. This is particularly a feature of non-League football, with amalgamations, reformations and so on, but the practice has been exercised at League level, notably by Orient. In 1898 they adopted the name Clapton Orient, which they used until

1946, when they changed to Leyton Orient. In 1966 the 'Leyton' was dropped, only to be restored in 1987.

Clapton Orient's programme from 1932/33 season also illustrates another point of interest with programmes through the years – a change in ground. The club played at Lea Bridge Road from 1930 to 1937, before moving to their present Brisbane Road, and it was to the former enclosure that Queen's Park Rangers journeyed on 12 November 1932. The club colours, as stated on the front cover, were 'Red and white hooped shirts, black knickers', to which were added blue and green to make a most attractive cover design – and no front page advertisements! However, the remainder of the sixteen pages were fairly run-of-the-mill, with no lack of adverts inside.

Bury programmes are amongst the rarest of pre-1960 items, including pre-war issues. In 1928/29 they issued a twelve-page programme with a pale blue cover overprinted in black. Internal pages were plain black on white. The format of the front cover – one third of adverts at the top and one third at the bottom, with content sandwiched in-between – is continued throughout the entire programme. There are items of interest in terms of text and statistics on every page, albeit overwhelmed by advertising above and below. Page eight contains an advert for watches, with the price ranging from £2 7/6d to £25. Another advert reads: 'When going to the match, order your taxi from The Central Carriage Company of Bury'. They must have had affluent supporters at Gigg Lane in those days to be able to go to matches in taxis!

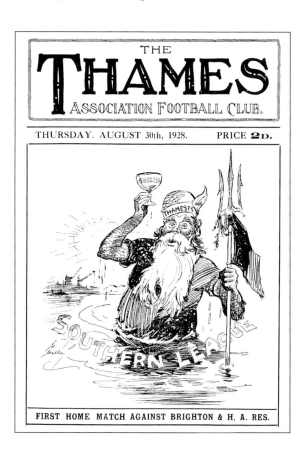

Thames were regular issuers of substantial programmes in their brief spell in the Football League, and even prior to joining it. This is their first home match, against Brighton and Hove Albion reserves in August 1928.

Left: *An attractive and colourful cover from Clapton Orient at Lea Bridge Road in November 1932.*
Right: *A rather plain-looking Bury issue from 1928/29.*

Some of the best pre-war programmes came out of Norwich, whose issues were attractive and entertaining. The third of their 1937/38 season issues was for the visit of Sheffield Wednesday in Division Two on 11 September (a fairly clear indication that City did not include reserve match issues in their numbering sequence). Yellow and black on a white cover, with no hint of the second colour of green, the thirty-two pages amounted to excellent value for 2d. The cover was headed by a sketch of Norwich Cathedral and the almost mandatory pre-war programme front cover advertisement was unusual in that it related to the home club – a local jewellers advertising 'Norwich City Football Club Cuff Links … finely enamelled in club colours, 10/6d a pair'. The programme was filled with facts and figures and the club notes, entitled 'Canary Seed', included many amusing anecdotes. An unusual and impressive five pages were given over to 'Our Visitors Today'. When collectors bemoan the standard of early programmes in comparison to the magazine-style issues of the 1980s and '90s, they should consider the exceptionally full programmes issued by the likes of Norwich City in the 1930s.

The history of football programme covers is littered with bad sketches of players. We have had the bad, the ugly and the repetitive, with most clubs at some time or another using the Lettraset-stock cartoons of footballers. Few, however, could match the sketch used by Chesterfield on the front of their 1937/38 programme. There is not even a front page advert – and no match details – to divert one's attention from the awkwardly poised and amateurishly drawn figure. Sixteen pages, slightly larger than A5, printed in blue on dull white paper throughout, this particular item was printed for a fixture with Sheffield Wednesday. Line drawings were used internally instead of photographs, so one has to question the modernity of the printer's equipment – even by contemporary standards. With the introduction of adverts to the front page, the Chesterfield cover improved post-war, but in common with most League issues, the content and scope of the programme did not return to its pre-war level for some decades.

It is often forgotten that Gillingham were once voted out of the Football League and the last match of 1937/38 season, played at Reading on 7 May 1938, was their last game in the League until they were voted back in for the start of the 1950/51 season. Unfortunately, there are not too many copies of *The Reading FC Record* around to satisfy the 'first and last' game collectors. The programme has eight large pages for one penny, with the cover pressed into service for League tables, as well as the usual advertisements for local businesses, cinemas and theatres. Page two had Supporters' Club notes, page three was entitled 'Wit and Humour' – which most readers would dispute given that the so-called jokes looked to be culled from Christmas crackers and the like – and page four had weekly comments, opposite the team line-ups on the other page of the centre fold. Page six trotted out 'A few football honours' and page seven had fixtures and results. Page eight had the half-time scoreboard surrounded by advertisements. The back page scoreboard, along with the front page lucky programme number and centre fold team lines, made it easy for the programme buyer to discover the basic information needed for a Saturday on the football terracing.

Left: *The stunning Norwich City issue from 1937/38.* Right: *This Chesterfield 1937/38 cover is as ugly as you are likely to see.*

The Cardiff City programme from 1936/37 was a brief, eight-page affair, printed in blue ink on stiffish white paper. Unusually for a programme of so few pages containing the usual advertising and statistical features, it carried a substantial two-page article from Onlooker.

There are not too many 1921/22 season Wrexham programmes that have survived the passing years and what makes this featured item even more noteworthy is that it is the first programme of the season – which was Wrexham's inaugural match in the Football League. The absence of match details on the front of the programme (strange in itself as there is editorial on that page) is compensated by the first reference of 'Our Notebook' by Argus: 'To-day, Saturday August 27th 1921, we make our debut as associate members of the Football League. Hartlepools United who provide us with our first match in the Third Division, come to North Wales with a great reputation.' Despite the unusual use of the front page for editorial, an advertisement still takes pride of place, and Soames' Welsh Ales are prominent over the years in Wrexham programmes, including those for international matches at the Racecourse Ground. This specimen is a real rarity and a piece of football history.

Unfortunately, one of the features of non-League programme collecting is that there is a steady supply of defunct clubs' issues, due to the high mortality rate in this grade of football. Some of the former clubs were amongst the top ones of their day, and most surviving programmes serve to keep their name alive and are historical documents of great interest and charm. There is also the continuous stream of name changes to add to the variety and interest of programmes. Take, for instance, a pre-war issue from Hampstead Football Club, who

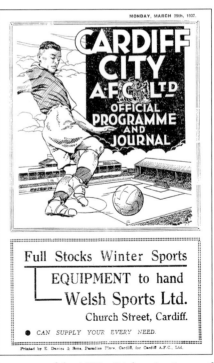

Left: *Reading opted for a functional front cover for the latter part of the 1930s.* Right: *A mixture of player and ground sketch was favoured by Cardiff City in 1936/37.*

Left: *Wrexham's first ever Football League programme.* Right: *Pre-war Hampstead – or was it old-name Hendon?*

played at Claremont Road, Cricklewood Lane, London NW2. This is the present day home of Hendon and a check on their history says that they were known as Hampstead Town from 1908 to 1933. Either they ground-shared with similarly-named Hampstead FC, or they had a minor name change en route. Tennis and cricket also came under the aegis of the club, as seen by the names and addresses of the respective secretaries for those sports as printed on the front page of the penny issue.

Ordinary programmes

Aside from issues of their favourite club, many collectors build up a fairly general collection of interesting and unusual programmes from other clubs. An interest in football in general is well served by a 'one per club per season' collection, in which the collector obtains a programme from every League club each season, either building up from current seasons or collecting one per club per season back to a specific year (such as 1980/81, 1970/71 or 1960/61). This is comparatively easy to accumulate, with very few instances of 'difficult' seasons for specific clubs, and it can be put together from various sources – club shops, exchanges and programme fairs as well as dealers' catalogues. The changes in a club's

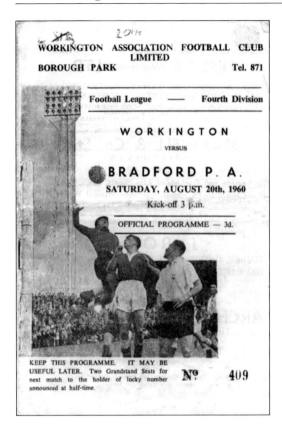

A one-per-club-per-season collection back to 1960/61 could include this meeting of two ex-League clubs, Workington and Bradford Park Avenue, on 20 August 1960.

fortunes and programme standards over the years make this a particularly fascinating collection. Should a club fall on hard times, such as Newport County **(13)**, Bradford Park Avenue **(14)**, Maidstone United or Aldershot, then a collection of this nature provides a good spread of issues of that club without the need to anticipate any difficulties which may befall them and make collecting their programmes of particular interest. One-off competitions, play-off matches, floodlight openings, friendlies, testimonials, ground openings, record scores, milestone matches for individual players – indeed, any match of note in a football historical context will provide a programme worthy of a place in any good general collection.

The introduction of the Conference at the top of the non-League 'pyramid' has produced another source of programmes, with the 'Fifth Division' producing programmes of a very high standard. For many years there was a brisk trade in pre-League programmes of clubs which gained election to the Football League (and by the same token, League programmes from the likes of Bradford Park Avenue, Workington, Southport, Barrow, Gateshead and others were also highly collectable) and this has now been extended by the automatic promotion and relegation place between the Conference and the Division Three.

The simple rule of putting together a good general collection is to keep an eye open for unusual programme issues, and attempt to obtain a programme from every football match and occasion of note; there is certainly no better way of marking such an occasion than by obtaining the appropriate match programme.

Wartime team sheets

It took football programmes about twenty years to recover from the Second World War, because it was not until the mid-1960s that programmes returned to the size and standard they enjoyed before 1939. The main setback came with wartime paper rationing and it is to the credit of most clubs that they continued to publish something during these difficult years, albeit it usually amounting to little more than a team sheet.

The initial confusion of early wartime football saw clubs issue greatly slimmed-down programmes, dropping to four or eight pages for Regional League matches in 1939/40. As the exigencies of war hit home, the programme shrunk again, to single or folded sheet issues. These constituted poor value for money for the buyers – they were invariably priced at 1d, only half the price of standard 1930s issues, which were certainly more than twice the size! A prime example of this was the excellent Queen's Park Rangers programme of 1939/40, weighing in at eight pages with a striking cover, which a year later was a single sheet with teams on one side and results and fixtures on the reverse.

Doncaster Rovers managed a four-page (folded sheet) programme for the first wartime season, this issue being for the game against Leeds. It was not long before Rovers were reduced to a single sheet.

Queen's Park Rangers were reduced to a single sheet for the 1940/41 season. This one was for the visit of Charlton Athletic.

Sheffield Wednesday settled for a single sheet (printed both sides) with barely a paragraph of text – in common with other programmes of the era, priority was given to team line-ups, results and fixtures, league tables and half-time scoreboard. Doncaster Rovers started off with a large four pager, but after a year dropped down to a single sheet, while Huddersfield Town and Leeds United strove heroically to sustain a four-page (folded sheet) programme. Rotherham, on the other hand, restricted their programmes to a single A5 sheet, printed both sides, with only a short paragraph of text.

The Leeds United wartime programme of 1942/43 amounted to little more than other programmes of the era – it was only a folded A4 sheet – but at least it contained something to read, with front page editorial stretching into the internal pages. Completing page two was a list of forthcoming fixtures, with matches against Barnsley, Huddersfield Town, Newcastle United and both Bradford clubs following that for the game in question, against Halifax Town. The team line-ups (printed in 2-3-5 formation) were above details of the next home match on Christmas Day – 2.45 p.m. *v.* Huddersfield: 'Make it a Present from "Santa" Bring the Wife and Kids!' – and included the clubs of guest players in the Leeds team (Harston of Barnsley, Moss of Aston Villa, Sturrock of Forfar and Rutherford of Glasgow Rangers). On the back page was a striking advert for Dunlop & Ranken ('For Everything in Steel'). This particular company was an enduring advertiser on that position over several decades at Elland Road. Printed in black on white paper, the cost of this programme was a steep 2d.

Manchester United settled for a single sheet which contained only results, fixtures and team lines and the same format was used, with the inclusion of some text and a little more information, by Millwall and Newcastle United.

One has to admire the dogged determination to carry on, despite the enormous disruption of the war, exemplified by these programmes. Team line-ups were obviously subject to great change as players came and went from the Forces, or were available from reserved occupations, and guest players abounded. Not the least of the attraction of these programmes is the existence of famous names in some unlikely team lists. Those few advertisers who remained in the greatly slimmed down programmes are fascinating. The four-page Sunderland programme of 1944/45, for instance, carried four adverts – George Younger's Prize Medal Ales, an encouragement to 'Shop at Binns for everything. Walk around any time – no obligation', a consulting optician and a local store which sold 'Radios, Bicycles and Prams, Re-conditioned Pianos and Utility Furniture'.

Wartime finals and representative matches

Just as clubs were subject to severe paper rationing, and had to reduce their programmes to single or folded sheets, so were the football authorities, despite being encouraged by the Government to keep football operating for the purposes of the nation's morale. Most cup finals and representative matches played during the war years were of this style and it was little short of scandalous that the authorities saw fit to charge 3d or 6d for these flimsy pieces of paper.

As with club football, normal international football was suspended, though the home international countries continuing to play one another in Red Cross internationals, with the gate proceeds going to war charities. There was a plethora of other representative games, mostly involving the various sections of the armed forces and small, single-sheet programmes were invariably produced for these matches. The RAF played Scotland at Hillsborough in November 1944 and a small four-page (folded sheet) programme was issued with a blue and white striped cover, priced at 1d. Pen pictures of both teams were included – the RAF forward line was Matthews, Carter, Drake, Mortensen and Smith (Brentford) while Scotland included the Liverpool pair Matt Busby and Billy Liddell. This illustrates the fascination of team line-ups in wartime programmes, with famous players popping up in the unlikeliest of fixtures **(15)**.

Scotland published a series of attractive little programmes which, although single sheets, were folded twice into narrow six-page issues. These were printed black and red on cream paper, and this splash of colour added some cheer to these otherwise meagre items **(16)**.

For England internationals and wartime finals at Wembley, the chosen colours were invariably patriotic red and blue, on white paper. The problem of paper supply was illustrated by a notice in the England *v.* Scotland match at Wembley in February 1944: 'Waste Paper Salvage … If you do not wish to retain this programme, or the part of your

Left: A plain cover for a plain, brief programme, when Arsenal met Charlton Athletic at Wembley in the War Cup (South) final in May 1943. Right: The blue and white stripes of the Sheffield Wednesday versus Blackpool War Cup (North) final in 1943 at least attempted to brighten up the sombre wartime years.

ticket you retain after entering the Stadium, please place them in any one of the many receptacles provided for clean waste paper as you leave the ground.' The programme was no more than a folded A4 sheet, making four pages, printed blue on white paper, with red spot colour added to one side **(17)**.

The 1943 Football League (South) War Cup final between Arsenal and Charlton Athletic at Wembley was a simple four-page production with a sketch of one of Wembley's towers on the front. Printed blue on white, it was somewhat pricey at 6d. Characteristic of these programmes was the 'Air Raid Precautions' warning on the front cover.

In contrast to the rather bland-looking Wembley programmes, the brief issues from the Northern half of England were at least brighter to behold. Sheffield Wednesday played host to Blackpool in May 1943 in the War Cup (North) final and the front cover of the folded sheet was printed with blue and white stripes.

The ingenuity of British forces abroad stretched to programme production, and there are many instances of Forces matches in Egypt and India which had brief match programmes produced, albeit featuring little more than the team line-ups.

Five
Cup-Tie Specials

Up for the cup

The magic of the cup, that special frisson of excitement which punctuates the weekly grind of League matches as winter takes its grip, is reflected in the collecting of programmes for cup-ties. The contents, scarcity and collectability of cup-tie programmes mark them out from normal League issues.

A cup-tie gives programme editors an excuse to look back on past cup glories and allows them to indulge in fantasies far removed from the reality of divisional position – asking the annual question 'Could this be our year?' When a bigger, more glamorous club comes to call, it is often the excuse to make an extra effort in terms of contents, cover design and size, and an increase in the number of pages, page size and, inevitably, the cover price!

Such 'specials' are subject to greater demand by both types of programme buyer – the casual purchaser at the match, who may not normally bother to purchase a League programme, but who is caught up in the cup-tie hype and the collector, who will attempt to purchase big match or special programmes as a priority over the hundreds of ordinary League issues. As a consequence of the first type of purchaser, there may be fewer surplus programmes to satisfy collectors who did not attend the match. As a result of the second, demand will be greater than normal for an already restricted supply of cup-tie programmes.

On the other hand, some clubs made do with their ordinary League programmes and these slim, flimsy issues were consequently less durable and are now extremely rare, few of them having survived the passing years. Yeovil Town were, and remain, formidable cup opponents for 'giants' fearing a 'killing'. Before 1945 they were known as Yeovil and

Petters, and it was in this guise that they entertained Liverpool at The Huish in an FA Cup third round tie on 12 January 1935. A substantial programme was issued by the non-League team – or more particularly by their Supporters' Club. No doubt this is a much-prized item for Reds supporters fifty-five years later.

As might be expected, these collectable issues will fetch higher sums than contemporary League programmes. For programmes in the 1990s and 1980s, there will be probably be a premium of 50p on the price of a League programme; £1 may be added for 1970s and 1960s League Cup and FA Cup issues, and expect to pay up to twice as much for 1950s and earlier cup-tie programmes as you would for League match programmes of a similar vintage.

Cup-tie programmes are an attractive set to collect because they come in manageable numbers. Rather than committing yourself to collecting up to twenty League matches a season, a handful of cup-ties each year will see the set completed far quicker – and to a much smaller budget. This would enable the collector with limited funds to spread the 'age' of his collection more widely and to add some expensive issues from the 1940s and 1950s, a few at a time. This could not be contemplated, financially, if every home programme were targeted, including League matches, when 1940s programmes are fetching upwards of £10 at auction.

By concentrating on the (comparatively fewer) cup-tie issues, the collector will be able to enjoy the competition of bidding by postal auction against other collectors, and the sensation of coming across a much sought-after programme by rummaging through boxes at programme shops and fairs, or in sifting through the pages of programme dealers' catalogues. Sometimes the hardest programmes to obtain don't involve a match played by your club, or are for slightly obscure fixtures out of the ordinary run of League and cup events. Thus, for Arsenal, Ipswich and Bournemouth fans, the folded sheet issue for the FA Cup first round second replay at Highbury on 1 December 1952 is never the easiest programme to obtain. Host club Arsenal issued a very much slimmed-down version of their medium-sized issue, in black print on white non-gloss paper, with red background colouration on the front page. Although there are no advertisements in the issue, it is questionable value at 3d. An Arsenal action shot was on the front cover and team line-ups and 'Voice of Arsenal' – in greatly reduced size – on page two. Comprehensive pen pictures of the two teams and three head and shoulders photographs from each camp filled the last two pages. Such neutral venue fixtures and the relevant programmes are now of course a thing of the past, with claims of overcrowded fixture lists and the strain of too many games for players.

When First Division Huddersfield Town visited Plainmoor in the fourth round of the FA Cup in January 1955, Torquay United issued a special souvenir programme, comprising sixteen A5 pages. The outer cover was on gloss paper and had red and yellow spot print, along with the black on white for the remainder of the programme. Page two had advertisements, whilst pages three, four and five each had four head and shoulders photographs of the visiting players. There was a full-page programme of music and community singing, opposite a half page of text – 'Plainmoor Calling!' by The Traveller. The centre spread featured the teams surrounded by adverts, then came pen pictures of both teams, top-and-tailed with small adverts. The Supporters' Club had a half page of

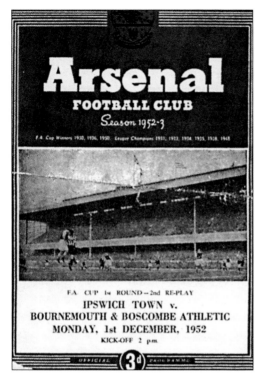

Left: *An FA Cup first round second replay – Ipswich versus Bournemouth. The programme and stadium were supplied by Arsenal.* Right: *Torquay United issued a special programme for the visit of Huddersfield Town in the FA Cup in January 1955.*

text, opposite the half-time scoreboard and brief Torquay statistics. Page fourteen had League tables and fixtures and results for the first team and reserves. The other three pages of the cover sheet contained advertising. This meant that not only was the standard Torquay programme dramatically increased in size, but that the price doubled to 6d.

Wigan Athletic, then of the Cheshire League, didn't make a special effort for their programme when Newcastle United visited in a third round replay in January 1954, although their brightly designed cover does suggest a cup-tie special (it was, in fact, the standard design for the Springfield Park club in the early 1950s). The programme was printed on one large sheet and folded twice to produce six pages, split (unevenly) between advertising, text and brief statistics. This form of production was very popular on either side of the war, avoiding the need to collate and staple multi-page programmes.

In Scotland, the qualifying rounds of the cup competition tend to eliminate the non-League clubs before the entry of the bigger clubs (at the third round stage as it is now known). There have been occasions in the Scottish FA Cup's history when the structure was changed to improve the chances of progression of a club from the Highland, East of Scotland or Southern League – and improve their chances of drawing one of the 'big guns'. One such occasion was in 1952/53, when Eyemouth United were drawn at home to Celtic in the first round on 24 January 1953.

Jock Stein, Bobby Evans, Bobby Collins, Willie Fernie and Charlie Tully were all in the Celtic team who visited Playing Fields Park in the Berwickshire coastal village. Not surprisingly, the home club marked the occasion by issuing a twelve-page non-gloss programme, mainly in black print, but with maroon print on page headings and many adverts. At a purchase price of six old pence it was expensive for its day, but the content served to offset the price charged. Page one had the match details and a photograph of the home side, page two contained the chairman's message, club details and two adverts, page three had a photograph of the Playing Fields Park stand and pen pictures of the Eyemouth United team, which were continued on pages eight and nine. Pages four and five had a 'Welcome to Celtic' with pen pictures, photographs and some advertisements, whilst the centre pages consisted of the team line-ups and adverts. Pages ten and eleven were mostly adverts interspersed with the half-time scoreboard and the music selection to be played by the local high school's pipe band and page twelve had a photograph of Eyemouth harbour with a narrative extolling the virtues of the small fishing port as an ideal holiday spot. There were also two small adverts on the reverse cover, one of which had Charlie Tully 'telling all' in the *Sunday Dispatch* newspaper. The programme was printed by J. Bain &

Left: An ordinary six-page programme for Wigan Athletic versus Newcastle United, FA Cup third round replay in January 1954. Right: The Eyemouth United team pose on the front cover of their programme against Celtic for a first round Scottish Cup-tie.

Left: A rare Scottish non-League versus League match in the cup programme in February 1954. Raith Rovers achieved their record score in this tie against Coldstream. Right: Nithsdale Wanderers versus Aberdeen in the Scottish Cup, February 1948.

Sons of Edinburgh and was reminiscent in style and content of the Heart of Midlothian FC programmes issued during the 1950s.

Eyemouth United issued for all their Scottish Cup-ties in the 1950s and 1960s when they were drawn against major Scottish League opposition and programmes exist for matches against East Fife and Kilmarnock. As with that featured game against Celtic, they are extremely rare and difficult to obtain. The club is no longer the force it once was, when not many senior sides relished a visit to their tight little ground which has long since been vacated. They now play at Gunsgreen Park overlooking the North Sea and programmes are occasionally issued for East of Scotland League fixtures, although the club is no longer a full member of the SFA and able to compete in the qualifying rounds of the Scottish Cup.

Just over a year later, First Division Raith Rovers also made a trip to the Borders, to play Coldstream in the second round on 13 February 1954. The Home Park (named after the local landowner, the Earl of Home, later Prime Minister Sir Alec Douglas Home) side were never one of the stronger non-League outfits in Scotland, and the 10-1 scoreline remains Rovers' record win in a national competition. The eight-page programme is printed blue on white, with team line-ups taking up the entire centre fold. There is a history of the visitors, pen pictures and a page three welcome. This item is quite a rarity now, although the 'Lucky Programme Number' on the top right-hand corner would point to a decent print run for a crowd of 1,100.

On the other side of Scotland, Nithsdale Wanderers of Sanquhar, Dumfriesshire, issued a souvenir programme for the visit of Aberdeen in the Scottish FA Cup second round in February 1948. Only four pages (an A4 folded sheet) on poor quality paper, the team line-ups are surrounded by adverts on the inside and there is a brief cup history on the back page. The programme, now very rare, was printed by the local newspaper, *The Cumnock Chronicle*.

Foreign issues set the post-war standard

England's humiliation at the hands of the Hungarians in 1953 and 1954 was the most vivid manifestation of the eclipse of British football by rising standards on the continent in the decade which followed the Second World War. In terms of football programmes, a similar trend had been evident long before Messrs Puskas and Hidgekuti displayed their skills.

The few continental programmes which found their way back to these shores after the war were years ahead of their UK counterparts, the latter struggling to shake off post-war rationing and restrictions and, more pertinently, lethargy and disinterest by their publishers. The contrast was greatest just across the Irish Sea. Irish Cup final programmes from 1945 to the late 1950s not only contained more pages than their Wembley or Hampden counterparts, but included less advertising and were half the price (3 Irish pennies, compared with 6d sterling). In May 1957, when England visited Dalymount Park to play Eire, the Shelbourne Supporters Club issued a twenty-four page programme packed with interesting features and articles the likes of which would not appear in many English programmes for another decade.

One of Manchester United's earliest European matches was in Dublin against Shamrock Rovers on 25 September 1957. The sixteen-page 6d programme produced by the home club was arguably superior to many of the programmes issued across in England at that time, including team groups, plenty to read and two pages of song lyrics for the pre-match community singing.

Even the poorest of continental programmes compared well with their British counterparts. Pre-communist Hungary issued twelve-page international programmes in black and white, but only two of the pages were advertisements. British programmes in the 1940s and 1950s were colourless in more ways than just the use of printers' ink, and full-colour cover illustrations were not to arrive on these shores until the 1960s – unlike Belgium, Holland and France for post-war international matches and, more spectacularly, in South America, where some countries issued colourfully designed and substantial issues for the visit of touring European countries.

As the 1960s loomed and the penny-dreadfuls (which actually cost 3d) remained in place throughout the game, issues from foriegn clubs put British programme producers to shame. In the late 1950s and early 1960s, the better clubs from England, Scotland and

Left: *Frankfurt XI versus League of Ireland in 1955, which opened the new Frankfurter Stadion.*
Right: *Hessen XI versus League of Ireland in 1955 at Kassel.*

Ireland were invited to play tournaments in Canada and the USA during the close season, and from these games emerged large, brochure-sized match programmes filled with photographs. From the early days of European club competitions came club newspapers and more substantial conventional programmes from the so-called undeveloped continental clubs. These examples from abroad, where programmes were not as much a part of the football fabric as they were in Britain, showed that the inadequate matchday programmes being offered within these shores were not so much a sign of the times, as an illustration of complacency and bad customer relations. Unfortunately, little was to change until the mid-1960s.

The widespread issue of programmes abroad is illustrated by a trip made in 1955 by the League of Ireland, and their series of matches against the Hessen League, one of the German regional leagues which pre-dated the establishment of the Bundesliga in the early 1960s. Frankfurt, as well as being the financial centre of the country, is also the capital of the German province of Hesse. On 14 May 1955 a League of Ireland selection met a Frankfurt XI to open the new Frankfurter Stadion. The German players were all drawn from FSV Frankfurt and Eintracht Frankfurt. A twenty-four page A5 brown programme greeted the spectators. While the football was the main event there was also athletics, handball and even a rugby exhibition to entertain the fans. A page of welcome and a page on the history of the stadium was included, with the remainder of the programme detailing the schedule and teams. The football line-ups occupied the centre pages, but over half of this (now very rare) programme was taken up with adverts.

Five days later the Irish made the journey north to Kassel to meet what appears to be a Hessen XI. The German side was selected from three clubs with four KSV (perhaps local club SV Kassel) players in the eleven. Seven players from the two Frankfurt clubs made up the team with four surviving from the first game. The Hessen XI won 5-0. The programme was a four-page A5 green issue with black writing. There wasn't one word of English in either programme, but the lengthy editorial in this case is mainly concerned with the Irish side, detailing their players, mentioning the forthcoming international between the two countries and giving an account of the game in Frankfurt.

Post-war penny dreadfuls

Thus rationing and the restrictions which forced clubs to abandon their sixteen to twenty-four-page programmes of the 1930s for the four-page or single-sheet issues of wartime, served only to provide an excuse for clubs to continue to neglect their programmes throughout the 1950s.

A club as big and as successful as Tottenham Hotspur, for instance, persisted with a four-page folded programme (albeit a large sheet) up to and including their double-winning 1960/61 season. In common with other major clubs from the capital, there was an absence of advertisements from the Spurs sheet, which meant that its content was no worse than the advert-laden eight- or twelve-page programmes issued by other clubs, but this merely confirms the poor standard generally, and the reluctance for clubs to improve their programmes when paper shortages and rationing were lifted.

Another successful team of the decade, Wolves, went through the 1950s with no more than eight pages in their programmes. Although these were brightly coloured and with a substantial article by a journalist in the centre pages, to modern eyes this was a wholly inadequate programme from such a major force in the game (18). Sheffield Wednesday issued only eight-page programmes in 1950 and (typically) were still doing so ten years later.

A curious aspect to this unsatisfactory state of affairs was that there was little distinction between the well-supported clubs in the First Division and the perennial strugglers in the two regionalised Third Divisions. Football was enjoying unprecedented popularity – in terms of attendances at least – in the immediate post-war years, but the massive crowds who watched League Championship winners such as Liverpool, Portsmouth, Tottenham and Wolves, as well as challengers like Bolton, Huddersfield, Preston, Newcastle and Blackpool, were subjected to no better programmes than those issued by Leeds United, then a struggling Second Division side (20), Torquay United (21), Oldham Athletic (22), York, Accrington Stanley, New Brighton, Bradford City (19) and Halifax (who in the same period had to apply for re-election to the League).

Programmes were in a vicious circle – few bought them because they were such poor value for money and because of low sales clubs refused to devote more time and expense to something that seemed to be more of an obligation than a benefit. Indeed, many,

Spurs made the effort – and an eight-page programme – to celebrate their return to the First Division in 1950.

including programme buyers, regarded their worth in terms of the team selections and half-time scoreboards. Little wonder that few other features were included by the vast majority of League clubs in the 1940s and 1950s.

Occasionally, even the poorest of programme producers could pull out the stops when it came to special fixtures. The notion that Spurs were one of the big clubs in English football was somewhat foreign to their fans either side of the Second World War. When the 1949/50 side won the Second Division championship, it had been fifteen years since White Hart Lane had witnessed First Division football. To celebrate, the Spurs directors issued a special eight-page programme for the final home match of the season against Grimsby Town on 22 April 1950. This was produced on light gloss paper, printed in black with lemon spot colour on some headings and as a background to photographs. The chairman and the editor pay tribute on pages two and three, and the welcome to Grimsby starts on the latter, finishing on page four. There are club notes and information on the two centre pages, along with team line-ups (in 2-3-5 formation) and a cartoon. Pages six and seven had pen pictures of the Spurs squad, along with full-length photographs of each player. The back page was laid out in the traditional fashion for a Spurs programme of this period – half-time scores, results, fixtures and league tables.

Collecting Tips: Cataloguing your collection

There are two major benefits to cataloguing one's programme collection. Firstly, this will indicate which programmes are still required to complete sets (and, by the same token, to ensure that the same programmes are not bought twice) and, secondly, this will form the basis of a filing and retrieval system to enable instant reference to a specific programme within a large collection. The chosen cataloguing system should be sufficiently flexible and 'open ended' to accommodate an expanding collection and should be capable of handling a collection of 500 or 5,000 or 25,000 items without modification. It should also interlink with the storage and filing system used.

The following example is one of a number of possible systems that may be used or modified to suit the individual collector's requirements. It is best to catalogue in speciality order. If your interest is home and away programmes of a favourite club, the catalogue should have lists of games played in a season, with a notation (a tick, for instance) when a programme has been added to the collection. Blanks indicate programmes still required, a cross would indicate that no programme was issued for a match (this is particularly useful information, as there is nothing quite so frustrating, or time-wasting, as searching for years for a programme which simply does not exist). The storage file of these programmes should correspond with the page in the catalogue. One-per-club-per-season collectors would normally file programmes in club order and on that basis a large schedule should be kept with club names down one axis and seasons along another. A tick should be used to indicate when a gap in that collection has been filled. A list of big matches played (such as internationals and cup finals) may be obtained from football text books like Rothmans *and* News of the World *annuals) and matches ticked off when programmes are received. These lists and catalogue pages should be sufficiently structured to allow for expansion with every new season, or with each earlier season collected. One other tip is to use a booklet or file of a style and size that can comfortably be taken to a programme fair and referred to with ease.*

Computers can greatly assist in cataloguing collections. A spreadsheet or database can be designed to suit the peculiarities of one's collecting habits, or there is an excellent Programme Collectors Database on the market which is easily installed and readily learned. It is also flexible enough to cater for most collecting idiosyncracies. At a later stage, we will describe an intensive cataloguing and reference system for an advanced programme collection.

The boring 1950s

With wartime rationing at an end, it took some time for clubs to recover the form and substance of their pre-war programmes. Football club programmes scarcely changed throughout the 1950s. The decade started with advert-laden eight- or twelve-page programmes in which photographs were a rarity and finished on the same note. For the vast majority of clubs, the format was predictable, beginning with a front cover with sketch of footballer or stadium, usually with advertisements. Very occasionally, there would be a photograph of the relevant ground.

There would be an editorial on page three which was often continued into other pages. This would give a review of recent matches and a preview of that day's fixture. The text was scarcely revelatory and was never controversial. It was usually the work of the club secretary who felt he had better things to do with his time than compile a match programme that would be bought by a small percentage of spectators. There was also an introduction to the visitors (usually consisting of pen pictures), match reports of recent first team and reserve eleven games (sometimes including narrative, otherwise just team selections). The rest of the programme would contain the half-time scoreboard, league tables, fixtures and results for first and second team matches, and not a great deal more – interrupted, of course, by the flow of advertisements. The team selections would invariably be in 2-3-5 formation on the centre pages, surrounded by small adverts.

This format was not only widespread, but it was also enduring. Most clubs issued only eight-page programmes in 1950 and were still doing so ten years later. Bournemouth, for example, issued an eight-page programme for the third year running in the 1955/56 season and, seven years later, a practically identical eight-page programme was issued, with the same cover design. There was only one substantial difference – the price had gone up to 4d. The contrast between these programmes of between forty and fifty years ago and today's glossy magazines could not be more stark. There were no policy statements from managers or chairmen, few features on star players, no coverage of commercial activities (for there were none to be reported on) and photographs were few and far between.

As a snapshot of the society in which the club was placed, however, 1950s programmes paint an instructive picture, thanks to the mass of advertisements and occasional editorial nuance. The omnipresent theatre advertisements, listing the current shows, which characterised most pre-war programmes were replaced with billings for the many cinemas in the towns and cities of Britain. Local breweries were prominent advertisers, as were the major industries of the locality. In pre-supermarket, chain-store and DIY superstore days, the multitude of small trader advertisements indicates a very different local economy to the one we know today.

Isolated excellence in the 1950s

Amid the plethora of twelve- or eight-page (and occasionally worse) advertising-dominated thin programmes of the 1950s, there were a couple of shining beacons of high quality, notably from the London pair Chelsea and Arsenal. The abiding thought is that if these two clubs could devote resources to produce excellent, interesting programmes, then why couldn't the other major clubs follow suit?

Pre-war, Chelsea had never been ones for expansive programmes, although their large sheet, blue print on white paper, four or eight pagers were always packed with information (and no adverts) and invariably enlivened with an attractive cartoon. They quickly changed tack after the war and by 1948/49 had established a substantial, conventional programme amounting to sixteen pages. This was filled with features, information and photographs, both action and portrait, which could simply not be found in other programmes. The programme went through a number of changes in design and presentation until it settled into a stylised sixteen-page issue in the late 1950s, but still with the same mixture of features and photographs, and plenty to read.

Like their London neighbours West Ham, Spurs and Arsenal, Chelsea eschewed advertisements in their match programmes until the mid-1970s, but it was only the

Gunners who matched the excellence of the Stamford Bridge programme two decades earlier. At first, Arsenal favoured a slightly larger page style, which was appreciated by supporters who enjoyed the substantial and authoritative writing. 'Voice of Arsenal' on the first two pages became a feature of a trip to Highbury and, like Chelsea, there was the novelty of a number of action photographs contained within the programme.

Arsenal reverted to a more conventional A5 size in the mid-1950s, but still the content remained of a high quality and quantity. There were always four action photographs spread across two pages (a rarity in 1950s programmes), a full page of pen pictures of the visitors opposite the team line-ups, a substantial article on general football matters (entitled 'Jottings by Spectator'), a team group photograph of the visitors (another rarity in programmes of the era) and a page on an aspect of the club's history. Added to the authoritative editorial were all the standard features of a programme.

Few clubs could match the standards set by the two London clubs, although Manchester United's 1950s programme could find few critics. Shorter in length (by four pages) than the Chelsea and Arsenal issues, and including some advertising presence, the United programme still offered more than the majority of 1950s programmes. There was a page of action photographs to complement the one on the front cover, a thoughtful piece by manager Matt Busby, two substantial topical articles by journalists and an entertaining full-page cartoon by Butterworth, entitled 'Bricks and Bokays'.

What the Arsenal, Manchester United and Chelsea programmes had in common was that someone had taken the trouble to devote time and imagination to their compilation, in contrast to the indifference towards their matchday issues shown by the majority of League clubs in the 1950s **(23, 24)**.

Six
Into Europe

EUROPEAN CLUB COMPETITIONS

Several of the most varied selections of collectable programmes come from the annual representatives in the three European club competitions and the continental clubs they are drawn against. The passing decades of European competition have broadened this into an opportunity for a substantial collection on its own, as hundreds of programmes have accumulated from the involvement of British clubs over the last forty years.

The vast majority of home match programmes, even back to the early 1960s, remain fairly readily available, and the less numerous issues from the late 1950s appear regularly, albeit on offers lists. While all of these programmes sell at a premium when compared to contemporary League issues, they can form a complete and substantial collection at comparatively modest cost. Difficulties begin to arise with programmes from the 'away legs'. In the first two decades of European football, before the spread of the hobby and establishment of dealers, very few match programmes were brought back to these shores. The only hope was the club shop, when someone had the gumption to organise fifty or so programmes to come back in the team hamper. This did not always happen and consequently many of the early programmes are extremely rare and eagerly snapped up by club collectors when they infrequently appear on offers lists.

This situation has eased considerably over the last twenty years as the programme trade has become more sophisticated and organised, with dealers either bringing programmes directly from the clubs, or arranging with travelling supporters to bring back sufficient quantities to satisfy the growing demand. The only price problem in this instance is the additional cost – firstly of purchase, not helped by exchange rates and different cost-of-living levels, and secondly of transportation. Consequently, you can routinely expect to pay no less than £3 (and up to £5) for a current or recent season, European away programme, irrespective of the quality of the issue – which can range from an enormous brochure to a glorified team sheet.

The majority of collectors confine their interest to programmes from their own country, but many Scottish, Irish and Welsh collectors extend to collecting English clubs in Europe, while a handful of real enthusiasts collect all British clubs in Europe. This has become particularly interesting in the last few years with the reform of UEFA competitions, and we now have a couple of Welsh League clubs issuing each season, where previously one of Cardiff City, Wrexham, Swansea City and the late-lamented Newport County would represent the principality as Welsh Cup holders (or runners-up).

Aside from the luck of the draw, forty years of European club competition have spread the scope of this part of collecting to include many clubs. Clubs currently outside the English Premiership to have issued programmes in Europe include Stoke City, Norwich City, Watford, Ipswich Town (who won the UEFA Cup and played in the European Cup), Burnley and a number of others. In Scotland there are issues from Raith Rovers, St Johnstone, Dunfermline Athletic, Partick Thistle, Airdrie, Dundee, Kilmarnock, Motherwell and St Mirren.

A feature of many European club competition finals played on the continent in the 1960s was the issue of two or more programmes – normally one from the host national association and another from the host club, otherwise known as the 'stadium edition'. There were two such programmes for the first neutral venue final to feature a British club – Athletico Madrid *v.* Spurs in the 1963 European Cup Winners Cup. The programme, issued by the Dutch FA, sported a front page cartoon by Dik (a regular feature of such programmes and standard Ajax issues through the years) with red, blue and black print on white gloss on the cover **(25)**. Inside, there are a further sixteen pages printed in black on poor quality white paper (almost newsprint in fact), in which there are welcomes in three languages, a Spurs team group, a photograph of Jimmy Greaves, an action shot of Dave Mackay, histories of both clubs, pen pictures of both clubs, a page of caricatures of some players and the referee (again by Dik), tournament results and a full-page photograph of Danny Blanchflower. There is also the curiosity – repeated in other Dutch FA programmes – of the team line-ups being reproduced on three separate pages, including the centre spread.

The 'stadium edition' for the fixture was called, appropriately, *Stadion Nieuws* and was produced by the host club Feyenoord. The cover has green and red spot colour, in addition to the black print on poor quality white paper of the entire programme. There are no match details on the cover, which is practically identical to all other stadium and Feyenoord programmes of the era. Contents of this sixteen-page issue include a welcome in three languages, a lengthy article about the match and the competing teams, centre page team line-ups (in 2-3-5 formation surrounded by adverts) and another lengthy article on the history of both clubs. There are at least ten pages of advertisements and no illustrations or photographs other than the adverts and the sketch of the stadium on the front cover. It is, in short, a disappointing issue, although this is reflected in the price (25 cents) which is exactly half the cover price of the Dutch FA edition which is a more substantial, less commercial and far more attractive edition.

Real Madrid met Stade Reims in the European Cup final of 1959 and the German Football Association issued one of their standard big match issues for the tie played in Stuttgart on 3 June. Thirty-six pages long and slightly wider than A5, the familiar cover illustration was in green and white, along with the black on white gloss paper of the outer sheet **(26)**. Internally, it was black on poor quality white non-gloss paper. It looks to be a substantial programme – there weren't many British programmes of thirty-six pages in the late 1950s – but many of the features were duplicated in German, Spanish and French. Thus, welcomes from the UEFA President, DfB President, and the Mayor of Stuttgart occupy up to page sixteen, along with advertisements. On either side of the centre spread team line-ups (spread across the double page in 2-3-5) was an article on the competition, followed in the second half by team photographs of Young Boys Berne, Atletico Madrid and the competing teams. There were five articles in German and four pages of every result in the European Cup since 1956.

Real Madrid's fifth successive European Cup final saw them beat Eintracht Frankfurt 7-3 in front of the largest ever European Cup final crowd at Hampden Park, Glasgow, on 18 May 1960. The Scottish Football Association, as host authority, issued their familiar big match programme, albeit bigger (at sixteen large pages) and more expensive (1/-) than usual. The front cover sketch of referee and captains tossing a coin, with Hampden Park in the background, was black and white on a red background, and red spot colour was used throughout the black and white internal pages **(27)**. The SFA President gave a welcome in three languages on page two, opposite the programme of pre-match entertainment for the huge crowd. There were two pages of pen pictures and head and shoulders photographs of either team, the President of UEFA had a message in three languages and there were full-page aerial photographs of the competing teams' stadia and a half-page article on the four previous European Cup finals. The centre page had the teams in 2-3-5 formation on a red background of a football pitch (a time-honoured SFA style), a trilingual greeting from the Lord Provost of Glasgow and four head and shoulder photographs of administrators. To modern eyes, this is a brief and inadequate programme, but it was a major production for 1960, matched only by the SFA for the biannual visit of England to Hampden Park. The programme is by no means as rare as the previous season's final (Real *v.* Rheims in Stuttgart), nor the following season's in Berne (Benfica *v.* Barcelona), and it can be purchased from leading dealers' sales catalogues at around £15.

Britain's first success in the European Cup came in 1967, when Celtic beat Inter Milan 2-1 in Lisbon. The Portuguese hosts issued a substantial A5-size programme which amounted to fifty-two pages **(28)**. The first nine pages of text were welcomes in four languages, then four pages were devoted to the history of Celtic (again in four languages), followed by head and shoulders photographs and statistical details of Celtic over two pages and a page on the match referee. This filled the programme to the centre spread, where teams were listed in formation – Celtic in 4-2-4, Inter in 1-3-3-3. The second half of the programme had similar coverage of Inter Milan, photographs of

A programme for a game that never was. Had there been a replay in the 1968 European Cup final, Arsenal would have issued this programme.

the respective clubs' stadia and details of Benfica's matches in the European Cup. Printed throughout in black on white semi-gloss, there was a slightly thicker glossy cover featuring the trophy and a silouette of the continent, with light blue and yellow colours added. The price was 5 escudos, although many copies brought back to the UK were overstamped with the dealer's original selling price of 2/6d. There has been an explosion in interest for this match programme in recent years, coinciding with the recovery of Celtic's fortunes, and the higher profile adopted by the European Cup final which has encouraged more people to collect this set of programmes. The upper limit of the price is currently £100, with the programme increasingly appearing on offers lists, as opposed to fixed price straight sale on major dealers' sales catalogues.

The following year, Manchester United became the first English club to win the European Cup, beating Benfica 4-2 after extra time at Wembley, who issued a very ordinary and somewhat nondescript small-page programme for the final (29). Only sixteen pages in length and overpriced at 1/-, the cover had the club crests in two red pennants, with writing in blue and black on a grey background. The President of UEFA had a message in three languages and each team had an introductory article, a full-page squad photograph and pen pictures of the players. There was a list of previous finals, all the results in that season's competition and a page of facts and figures. Even the team lists were restricted to one page, in what was probably the poorest European Cup final programme ever seen. The familiar advertisers were present – *Radio Times*, Double Diamond and Bovril.

The 1999 Champions League victory by Manchester United has resulted in an explosion in interest for the 1968 final programme, which for many years has been readily available. A year ago, the price range was between £2.50 and £5, but that is moving upwards. Buy soon and, if you get the opportunity, try to seek out the first edition of the programme, printed before the game and available at the stadium. There is also a reprint in circulation, in which photographs are darker than the original.

An interesting aside to this fixture was that a programme was prepared for a potential replay, to be played at Highbury on 31 May. This was to be a standard small, sixteen-page Arsenal programme of the era, with a red background on the cover, otherwise black print on white paper. Advert-free, contents included articles and statistics on both clubs, team groups and previous match action.

In 1969, there was no absolute guarantee that every European club final would see a match programme produced and, coupled with the notorious reluctance of Spanish clubs to issue, there were fears that the Ajax *v.* AC Milan European Cup final would be

An unexpected delight – Ajax versus AC Milan, the 1969 European Cup final in Madrid.

programme-less. Such fears were groundless and the host club issued a substantial twenty-eight page programme, slightly larger than A5. The internal pages were black print on poor quality paper (almost newsprint) and the cover was printed blue, yellow and red on white gloss. The editorial was in both English and Spanish, with nothing in Dutch or Italian. Features included an introduction to the match, history of Ajax, head and shoulders photographs of both teams over three pages each, features on Rinus Michels, Johan Cruyff, Gianni Rivera and Nereo Rocca, champions of four other sports, previous finals, route to the finals and line-ups (in 4-2-4) all in the centre pages. The second half included a history of Milan, six action photographs – including two from English internationals, and a pictorial feature on Gento the former Real star.

By the time Liverpool were seeking their third European Cup final victory, the match programme had graduated into a glossy, colourful brochure. For the match with Real Madrid in the Parc de Princes, Paris, on 27 May 1981, the French Football Association issued a forty-eight-page A4 brochure, although the full colour was restricted to the outer cover (the inside pages of which were blank) and a number of internal advertising pages. Introductions from various dignitaries and a history of the competition dominated the start of the programme, each article being reproduced in three languages. The two teams had a page each, featuring pen pictures, a team group and a separate page with head and shoulders photographs of some of the players. Three pages referred to that season's cup competition and previous finals, and on the back page was a black and white aerial photograph of the venue. By British standards, this was a poor programme even for that era, but France have never been renowned for being enthusiastic programme producers, and the 10 franc cover price was reasonable.

Ipswich Town have enjoyed two golden spells in their history – the Bobby Robson years in which they won FA and UEFA Cups, and the Alf Ramsey era in which they won the League Championship and gave a good account of themselves in the following season's European Cup. In the second round, Italian giants AC Milan came to Portman Road and Town abandoned their pocket-sized programme and produced an A5 twenty-eight-page special. Printed black on white gloss, with spot colours of red and blue on the front and back covers and page three, content has been expanded accordingly with a lengthy introduction by Alf Ramsey, a report of the first match in Milan, photographs of the visitors, both team groups, pen pictures of both teams and supporters notes. The latter piece retains the feel of a normal Town programme, as does the list of that season's fixtures, although the format is undoubtedly in the 'special issue' class. The back page has an unusual design in red, black, blue and white, with portraits of the respective captains, Andy Nelson and Cesare Maldini. By modern standards there is not an enormous amount to read, but in 1962 this extended issue would have been deemed good value for the 1/- cover price.

One of the most eagerly anticipated European ties was the meeting of Celtic and Leeds United in the semi-final of the European Cup in 1970. The champions of England were in the midst of dominating the game south of the border, while Celtic's pre-eminence in Scotland was matched by their European Cup final victory three years earlier. After a 1-0 Celtic win at Elland Road, the teams met at Hampden Park, Glasgow, for the second leg in April 1970. For this competition, Celtic abandoned their

A special Ipswich Town programme for the visit of AC Milan in the 1962 European Cup.

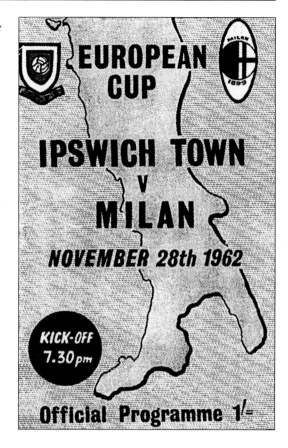

rather ordinary League match programmes and produced large-sized European issues, often keeping the same sketch of two players on the front cover but changing the two colours to match the visitors **(30)**. Thus the front cover was green and blue on white gloss paper, and inside the eight-page issue was a welcome to Leeds United, a team group photograph and a history of the club in words and statistics. There was also a list of European Cup finals and Inter Continental Cup-ties. In the centre pages the teams were laid out on a green pitch grid and there were photographs of the Celtic chairman and their manager, Jock Stein, along with three or four notes on the fixture. There were two pages of pen pictures of Leeds United, accompanied by photographs of Revie, Bremner and Charlton, and more miscellaneous notes. The only advert in the programme was on the back page, for Black and White Scotch Whisky. The programme is in plentiful supply, but increasingly sought after as the years roll on, and you may expect to pay at least £5. The first leg at Elland Road is slightly rarer, by virtue of a smaller print size for a smaller crowd, and sells for one or two pounds more.

As our story of the development of programmes nears the modern era, so programmes become more plentiful and therefore cheaper to buy. It is now appropriate to pause in order to examine the various ways in which a collector can add to his or her collection.

Collecting Tips: Buying from dealers' catalogues

By far the most prolific source of the items needed by collectors to complete their sets are programme dealers' catalogues. These are lists, in speciality order, of programmes for sale. Rarer items are put on offer, with the dealers conducting a postal auction, each programme going to the highest bidder. The collector's choice of dealer is very important. The majority are people of great integrity who have a depth of knowledge of the hobby. Sadly, as in all walks of life, there are a minority who are less scrupulous. Established dealers often advertise in specialist hobby magazines, such as Programme Monthly, *and may well advertise how long they have been in business. Some ask for 40p, 50p or 60p to cover the cost of posting out their catalogue, which can be in excess of sixty pages in length. One clue as to the status of a dealer is the frequency with which he publishes his catalogues – those who issue six or more in a year are likely to have vast, rotating stocks and are more likely to have new items of interest on each catalogue. Once in receipt of a catalogue, read the instructions carefully and, when ordering, or placing offers for programmes, follow the published instructions. One of the unfortunate aspects of buying by mail order is that you do not view the condition of the programmes (as you would, for instance, in buying at a programme shop or programme fair). Dealers try, as much as possible, to give accurate descriptions of programmes on their catalogues (whether they are folded, torn, creased, soiled or written on) but one man's good condition can be another's unsatisfactory state of repair. The best of mail order dealers operate a 'full refund if not satisfied with condition' clause which collectors with a genuine grievance should exercise, but very quickly – usually within a couple of days – following receipt of the unsatisfactory item. Other important tips are: shop around to familiarise yourself with the catalogues on offer and prices charged and don't spend (or offer) more than you can afford. Above all, don't worry too much if you miss out on a programme – another copy will certainly appear on the market in the fullness of time.*

Collecting Tips: Buying at programme fairs

The social medium for programme collectors is the programme fair, which serves an important dual purpose of also being an ideal means of viewing and buying programmes. Organised at least once a year in most areas of the country, fairs are patronised by up to a dozen stallholders comprising local or national dealers and local club shops. They display and sell a selection of their stock and are particularly useful to collectors of clubs in the immediate vicinity of the fair. An out-of-town national dealer will bring along his entire stock of programmes of local clubs, thereby filling a number of gaps in collections. For those with a passing interest in big match programmes and those of other categories, a fair is ideal for filling gaps in a collection and it is also a perfect vehicle for introducing fresh facets of collecting.

If you have, for instance, pursued a collection of one club's programmes and are down to the last twelve from the past thirty years, you will find that additions to your collection are very slow to come by. Perhaps a little bored by this lack of active collecting, you may hanker after the fresh stimulus which another category of collecting would bring (such as non-League, another club's homes, European competitions or internationals). A fair, with such a variety of programmes for sale, provides an ideal kick start for such a tangent to a collection. It is also an excellent starting point for the hobby, with many of the better stallholders selling bargain bundles (ten programmes for £2, for example), which gives a young collector a small number of big match and glamorous club programmes to set alongside his locally acquired first few issues. Local fairs are advertised in advance in the local press and club programmes, and the specialist press carries advance notice of programme fairs throughout the country.

Like the local club or programme shop, fairs have the advantage of putting collectors in contact with one another. A programme collection is a very individual thing, unique to the interests and football spectating habits of the collector, and is often accumulated in a relatively solitary and independent manner. Despite this, the hobby can be the catalyst of a wide range of friendships and contacts with football followers of varying persuasions throughout Britain and abroad. At a local level, collectors have a number of opportunities to meet and assist one another in their collections. Because of the individual aspects of collecting, there is no unhealthy competition and there is a remarkable level of co-operation between collectors with similar interests. A club shop is an ideal means of coming into contact with other collectors, with the programme counter manager often acting as a focal point in bringing collectors together. Meeting before a match, collectors can exchange notes and, of course, programmes. Some towns and cities have a programme shop, or stalls at open markets, run by a local programme dealer. These, again, are meeting places for collectors where points of mutual interest may be discussed. Occasional programme fairs bring a wider circle of collectors together, and more active and enlightened collectors occasionally organise collectors' meetings on a monthly or bi-monthly basis. These programme clubs vary from informal gatherings to properly constituted organisations.

The UK Programme Collectors Club is free to join and exists primarily to publish a register of members, by which collectors may obtain contact addresses and telephone numbers, cross-referenced to collecting specialities, of other collectors. A small charge is made for the register. Information and an application form may be obtained from UKPC, PO Box 3236, Norwich, NR7 7BE. While buying programmes from shops, fairs and by mail order will provide the bulk of a collection, those final, elusive issues are most often obtained from fellow collectors, either by purchase or exchange. It is important, therefore, to communicate with fellow collectors to keep abreast of changes in the hobby, new or obscure programmes on the market and, most importantly, to work to mutual advantage towards completing programme collections.

Inter-League matches

This may sound like an obscure and uninteresting category of programmes to collect, but thirty years ago no self-respecting collector would omit Inter-League matches from their big match collection. Now, the matches rarely rate a mention even in the history books, but the programmes form a fascinating set to collect at reasonable prices, as their diminishing supply is offset by the fact that there are few new collectors of this category.

The bulk of the programmes come from an annual round-robin series of matches between the Football League, Scottish League, Irish League (Northern Ireland) and League of Ireland (Eire). Matches were in midweek and, in England's case, almost always at provincial grounds. Scotland tended to keep the matches in Glasgow, although not always at Hampden, while the visits of the Scottish League and Football

League to both sides of the Irish border attracted sufficient crowds to warrant the use of recognised international stadia. The League of Ireland *v.* Scottish League match in September 1957 was one of a series played at Dalymount Park, Dublin, and a twelve-page programme was sold for 3d **(31)**.

Programmes were always issued, with Scotland and the two Irelands invariably producing contemporary big-match programmes which owed their origin to the governing body, rather than the host club. The large page size programme issued for the Scottish League *v.* English League match at Hampden in March 1967 was standard for its time north of the border. It contained twelve pages, printed blue with spot red on white gloss paper, and each team was given two pages of substantial pen pictures, with a scattering of head and shoulders photographs. Four or five fairly substantial articles on the fixture and its history, added to previous fixtures and that evening's fixture details, completed an informative programme. In England's case, in common with full internationals played away from Wembley, the responsibility for programme production lay with the host club.

Thus, we have matches against the Scottish League at Middlesbrough (1950, 1968 and 1972), Coventry (1970), Sunderland (1964), Newcastle (1948 and 1958) and

An attractive and informative big match programme was issued by the Scottish League for the visit of their English counterparts to Hampden Park in 1967.

Maine Road, Manchester (1974). In 1962, Villa Park was the venue for the match against the Scottish League and a standard twelve-page *Villa News and Record* was sold for 3d **(32)**. Villa maintained their tradition of numbering the internal pages from the start of the season, so this issue had pages 271 to 282, being the thirty-fifth issue of the nineteenth volume. Contents included Villa statistics, pen pictures and head and shoulders of the two teams and the usual advertisements.

The Irish League visited Norwich (1970 and 1963), Plymouth, Newcastle, Blackpool, Wolverhampton and the two Liverpool grounds between the war and 1970. Their southern neighbours visited Preston, Wolverhampton, the two Liverpool grounds, Leeds, Blackburn, Bristol City, Hull City and Barnsley.

The fixture between the Scottish League and Football League was a long-standing one and programmes from pre-war matches exist. Few survive – and in many cases none were issued – for matches North of the Border, but many have survived from England, most notably for matches played at Chelsea's Stamford Bridge. These often appear on offers lists and can be obtained for comparatively modest sums (no more than, and often less than, one would pay for a League match programme of that era).

There were other, one-off fixtures played by the Leagues over the years. The Football League played the Italian League twice in Italy, and in 1962 at Old Trafford and 1963 at Highbury; Football League select elevens have played matches in England and abroad, particularly after the Premiership split.

However, these fixtures were never part of a series, and they are of interest to representative match collectors only as one-off big match programmes, and are priced accordingly.

Seven
Domestic Variations

The first League Cup competition

We have mentioned earlier in this book that League Cup (now the Worthington Cup) programmes are an attractive series to collect, as they stretch back 'only' forty years, since the competition was launched as comparatively recently as 1960/61 season. A most interesting sub-set to collect are programmes from the first ever League Cup competition, but be warned – many of these are much sought-after by collectors and fetch inordinately high prices in offers.

The reason for this is that the competition was not taken terribly seriously in its early years and many clubs adopted a half-hearted attitude in the first season. Upsets, according to League position, were numerous and many of the larger clubs anticipated the lower attendances the struggling competition attracted and printed programmes to suit. There are, therefore, many single sheet and folded-sheet programmes, as clubs thought the competition unworthy of a full programme and, while the limited print runs probably satisfied those who attended the match, it meant that fewer have survived for collectors almost four decades later. Even if a collector's ambitions do not run to a full set of these programmes, it is worth keeping an eye out for them as most are now quite valuable.

Take, for instance, the Exeter *v.* Manchester United match. City issued a full programme, but it is now much sought-after, particularly by the army of United collectors. The replay at Old Trafford, a twelve-page effort, is not particularly scarce, but will still fetch four or five times the price of a 1960/61 League programme. Coventry issued a four-page programme for the visit of Barrow in the first round and this is now extremely scarce, as is the four-page Everton programme for the visit of Accrington Stanley: just 18,246 attended the match, compared with Everton's average of 43,450. Accrington played just two League Cup games before they resigned from the League, the other being at Lincoln in 1961/62. The programme from that game is an even rarer single sheet!

The first ever League Cup final programme, Rotherham United's home leg against Aston Villa in 1961 – played at the start of the following season.

In the first round, Bolton drew 0-0 at Hull, who issued a sixteen-page programme, while Wanderers issued an eight-page production for the replay, which they won 5-1. In comparison with others that season, the Burnden Park programme is not particularly difficult to obtain, nor is the second round tie against Grimsby Town (another eight-page affair). In the third round, Bolton set the ground attendance record at Feethams, as Darlington issued a full sixteen-page programme. Expect to bid up to £10 for that one, although the home side printed according to a massive 20,724 all-ticket attendance. Bolton's initial League Cup run came to an end at home in the fourth round, with eventual finalists Rotherham United winning 2-0. This was marked with another eight-pager, which is only slightly harder to obtain than the other two home programmes that season.

Both legs of the final, Aston Villa *v.* Rotherham United, are now 'offers category' programmes, with bids in excess of £100 likely to secure. Both teams issued no more than their standard League programme issue for the fixture.

Among many other programmes from that season's competition to look out for are Burnley *v.* Nottingham Forest on 19 December (postponed) and 10 January, both of which see bids starting at £20; Portsmouth *v.* Chelsea in the fourth round, an extremely rare single sheet; Southampton *v.* Leeds in the same round; and, one of the rarest in the entire competition, Chesterfield *v.* Leeds from the third round. The lattermost match kicked off at 2.15 p.m. and attracted only 2,021 spectators, but the four-page folded sheet will now fetch offers in excess of £100.

The mini – car, skirts and programmes

The early 1960s saw the prefix 'mini' applied to many of the period's innovations, not least the revolutionary popular car and the fashionable skirt. The mini vogue found its way into football programmes, with a number of English clubs, both in the League and at non-League level, favouring a small, pocket-sized match programme, quite unlike anything that had gone before or has appeared since.

Page sizes were square, ranging from 11 to 14 cm, and there were a variety of cover designs. Northampton Town and Swindon featured their club crests, while Barnsley, Southend United and Reading had either match action photographs or an aerial shot of their stadium. Torquay, as was their preference with larger programmes, featured a tourist-brochure photograph on their cover **(33)**. Rochdale preferred a sketch of two players and Crystal Palace doubled that number **(34)**. Orient and later Crystal Palace featured plain, but attractive designs which drew attention to the white gloss paper. Gillingham and Bradford Park Avenue used sketches of their main stands. Very few cover designs changed from match to match and a number of them didn't even include match details, to the annoyance of future generations of programme collectors.

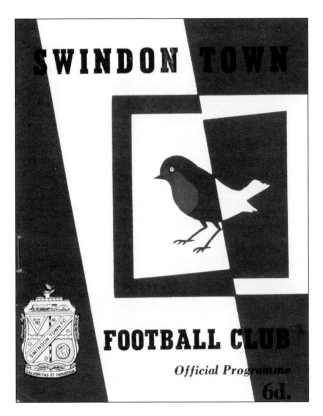

The red robin motif of Swindon Town featured on the club's mini programme in 1965/66.

Bradford Park Avenue's 1960 mini programme cover was devoid of match details, but featured a green, black and white sketch.

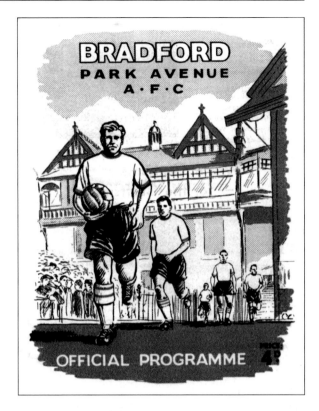

Non-League clubs who used the pocket-sized format included Bath City, Chelmsford, Corby Town, Worcester City, Margate and Guildford City. The earliest mini programme appeared to pre-date the car or skirt – Crystal Palace pioneered the format in 1957/58 and the last to use this style was Orient in 1968/69. Content was little better than contemporary programmes, with half of the pages given over to advertising, which was mostly local. There was an editorial, visiting team coverage, first team and reserve statistics, supporters' club notes, the occasional feature on a home player and very few photographs. Their passing, by the middle of the decade, could not be mourned in terms of their content or value for money (some were priced at 3d, others rather poor value at 6d) but to modern eyes they are a very attractive and fascinating novelty in the current sea of bulky, glossy, colourful programmes.

One of the major benefits of this style of programme is that they have survived the passage of time remarkably well. They did not need to be folded to go in a pocket and many of them sported a thicker, light card cover for added protection.

Some early 1960s surprises

Programmes did not emerge from their post-war slump in standards until after the 1966 World Cup, but as in any walk of life, there were rare beacons to illuminate the gloom for early 1960s programme buyers. The continued excellence of some of the major London clubs' programmes will be explored in the next chapter, but this was matched only in isolated instances elsewhere in Britain.

In Scotland, a notable exception to the rule of indifference was in the capital city, where both Hearts and Hibernian produced excellent programmes from the war until the early 1960s. Hibs, in particular, enjoyed splendid large-page issues, with thoughtful, informative editorial, an attractive design and plenty of photographs. Indeed, it could be argued that the Easter Road programme was just about the best in Britain in the 1950s. Hearts stuck with an A5 format throughout the 1950s and '60s, and in content and presentation produced another of the best programmes of that period. They were not averse to using Edinburgh's tourist attractions for their cover design.

An unlikely outpost for programme excellence was Barrow, now in the former Northern Premier League, but then a perennially struggling Third or Fourth Division club. The Holker Street issue was unexceptional in looks – for many years the front cover never changed from its stark dark blue and white advert-dominated basic design which contained no match information. Inside, however, there was unsurpassed value for money in an enormous article by 'Chatter Box'. This ran for up to seven or eight pages, consisting of paragraphs of news and comment presented without headings or illustrations. Aesthetically pleasing it was not, but it made for an excellent read.

The large page Hibs programmes of the early '50s were ahead of their time – and prolific too. This was an issue for a minor local cup-tie.

Left: *The Scott Monument in Princes Street takes pride of place in this Hearts versus Celtic programme from September 1964.* Right: *This Barrow programme looks the same as its predecessors over a long period, but there was plenty to read inside.*

Fulham's programme in the 1960s matched the team – unheralded in comparison with its larger London neighbours, but clinging doggedly to top flight status. There was always plenty to read in the Craven Cottage programme, which was one of the first to introduce full colour to the front cover. Not far away in West London, Eric White had taken over the Brentford programme and had begun to impart his love for the Bees through its pages. Times were hard at Griffin Park in the 1960s and the programme was by necessity a slim volume, but the reader-friendly Bees programme, some thirty years under White's influence, was beginning to emerge.

Portsmouth made an effort to improve their programme in that period, with a determination to provide more candid articles from manager and players. In common with the majority of their counterparts throughout the English and Scottish League, Pompey could not justify an increase in size or pages, and modern print and design techniques were expensive and in their infancy. However, they recognised that giving more thought and imagination to the contents could easily make the programme more attractive to potential buyers.

Such considerations were not shared amongst the major clubs. The programmes of the Manchester, Liverpool, Sheffield and Birmingham clubs could not be considered the worst in the League, but they were predictable, changed little with each passing season and performed only the rudimentary functions. It took the 1966 World Cup to galvanise clubs into action towards improving their image and catering for their supporters' needs.

Portsmouth were early programme innovators in the 1960s, as this attractive cover design from 1968/69 suggests.

There will be several crossroads which a collector will meet as their programme collection builds. As he or she exhausts the list of programmes which are readily obtainable, or as prices get beyond his or her pocket, a decision has to be made on the future destination of the collection. Does the collector expand his collection back in time, inevitably involving greater expense, or should it be expanded 'horizontally', by indulging a passion for football and compulsion to collect by branching into other categories? These alternative collection themes are many in number and we will attempt to give a flavour of some of them now.

Other Leagues

Once the collector has obtained at least one programme from each Football League club, he may wish to widen his one-per-club horizons to include clubs from other Leagues. Most football fans admit to an interest in a Scottish League or Irish League club and a logical next step would be to obtain a copy of each club's programme from one or both of these leagues. Nowadays, these are readily available with most good dealers carrying fairly substantial stocks, although the countries themselves have their own specialist dealers. There is a growing interest in Welsh league football and many of the principality's clubs have issued at their non-League level since the war. An early example is Bala, who produced a 3d programme for the visit of Shrewsbury Town, then in the Midland League, for a Welsh Cup-tie in December 1946.

A word of caution to those wishing a one-per-club-per-season collection in Scotland or Ireland. It is only comparatively recently that all clubs have issued every season, indeed some in the Irish League continue to go through a whole season without issuing a single programme. In Scotland, there have been some surprising omissions over the last twenty years, including a number of seasons in which Cowdenbeath, Montrose and Clydebank did not issue. Indeed, Clydebank did not produce programmes for their First Division campaign in the 1999/2000 season. Into the 1960s and '70s there are more gaps, while programmes were often a rarity in the Scottish Second Division in the 1940s and '50s.

One of the most fascinating tangents to explore in programme collecting is that of non-League programmes. Those from clubs in your vicinity are likely to be easiest to obtain. It should be noted that many non-League clubs have shops which boast programme stalls that are enthusiastically run and a marvellous source of non-League issues. Non-League programme collecting would warrant a book of its own, such is the length and depth of diverse programme production at that level of our sport. An early – but by no means the earliest – example is from Catford Southend in 1921/22. The club's title should perhaps have been

Collectors of Welsh programmes may wish to have an issue from Bala. This one was for a Welsh Cup-tie against Shrewsbury Town in December 1946.

written as South End, as they were firmly based in Catford, south-east London, nowhere near the Essex estuary town. Known as the 'Kittens', they were regular programme producers in the Kent League in the 1920s.

There are three main categories of non-League collecting: one per club, which is an endless and enjoyable task as there are always new issues amongst the thousands of non-League clubs, while the expanding Sunday scene is now spawning programmes of a good quality. Secondly, there are non-League friendlies against League clubs, which are mostly pre-season games and not always against first elevens. Thirdly, there are the annual jousts between non-League and League clubs in the first few rounds of the FA Cup. Dealers make a point of obtaining this latter category, which produces a wide variety of fascinating programmes, often from unexpected non-League qualifiers.

The itinerant Corinthian Football Club, an illustrious name from football's past, played their 1937 FA Cup first round tie against Southend United at the now-demolished White City Stadium, Shepherd's Bush. The programme comprised eight pages, printed in blue on off-white paper. Page two had club notes and an introduction to Southend, whose manager was David Jack, formerly of Bolton and Arsenal. They were referred to as 'not one of the most fashionable clubs in the South'. Page three had potted biographies of the visiting players; pages

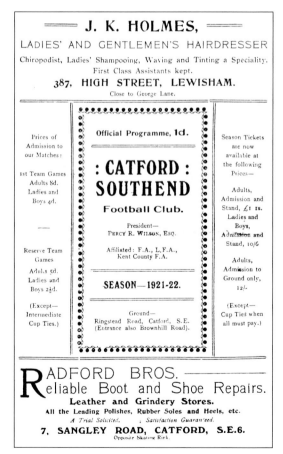

A 1921/22 programme from long-defunct Catford Southend.

A late excursion into the FA Cup proper for the famous old Corinthian Football Club in 1937.

four and five displayed the line-ups and pages six and seven information on the Corinthians. Page eight had the ubiquitous half-time scoreboard. Corinthian later merged with another famous non-League club, Casuals, and the combined club are still prominent at that level.

Foreign programmes

Enthusiastic collectors' clubs are run from Holland, Germany and Scandinavia, but the real hotbed of programme collecting is to be found in the British Isles. Despite the European single market and the so-called shrinking globe, there is still a reluctance for programme collectors to embrace continental programmes. The exception to this is when British clubs play in European competitions and when clubs undertake friendly matches abroad. A brisk market for such items exists, with dealers and club shops making special arrangements to import sufficient quantities of programmes. While these are invariably expensive in comparison with domestic programmes, buying from dealers is considerably cheaper and more convenient than attempting to obtain programmes direct from the foreign clubs.

The best method of obtaining domestic programmes from overseas is by befriending a programme collector in another country. These people often write to British clubs, who in turn print their requests for new friends in their match programmes. A few of the continent's more prominent collectors make themselves known to British dealers, programme magazines and clubs, and they are invariably willing to assist, where possible, in obtaining foreign programmes for British collectors.

Purchasing programmes direct from clubs on the continent is comparatively difficult. British postal orders or cheques are unlikely to be accepted and the main 'currency' in such matters is international reply coupons, which are obtainable at any post office at a cost of around 40p each. These, in turn, may be redeemed at any foreign post office for the cost of postage back to Britain. If you have obtained the address of a foreign club, a request for programmes should be accompanied by four or five international reply coupons in lieu of payment. As stated before, however, such a method of obtaining programmes from abroad is painfully slow and unreliable. Using contacts within programme collecting and searching for issues in dealers' lists are the best ways of obtaining foreign issues for your collection. For the specialist collector, it could be a fascinating sub-set of their collection. Just as in this country, there is a long history of programme production in certain countries of Europe, particularly to the north.

The Ullevi Stadium in Gothenburg produced fairly substantial sixteen-page programmes in the 1950s, for whatever club used it as home. Four colours were used in the light card cover, the issue contained head and shoulders photographs and, sadly and prominently, plenty of advertisements.

GAIS versus Helsingfors at the Ullevi Stadium, Gothenburg, Sweden, in July 1959. It is a sixteen-page programme as good as most in Britain at the time.

By the early 1970s, Swedish programmes had become much more sophisticated and when Orgryte played Malmo in April 1973, the programme, at forty-four pages, was much larger than anything produced at the time in Britain **(36)**. The issue was, however, again dominated by heavy advertising.

Collecting Tips: Advanced cataloguing

The more attention you give to your collection, the more enjoyment you will derive from it. Those who like to lavish a great deal of time on their pastime, and who have a bent for organisation and administration, can devise cross-reference systems for their collection which will cover all eventualities. This extreme form of cataloguing will not be to the taste of every collector, but there may be elements in the all-embracing system about to be described which can be used by most collectors in their chosen filing or cataloguing system. First of all, each programme is numbered as it enters the collection (sequentially, from one upwards). As every programme is inserted into its own polypropylene bag (or paper bag, or envelope) a small adhesive label with the number written on is attached to the top right-hand corner of the bag. A ledger of each programme's details is kept in numerical order, recording competing teams, date of match, cover price, date bought and amount paid. Next, the programme's details are recorded in a master catalogue, with a page (or pages) for each home club or category (England internationals, England under-21s, FA Cup finals, testimonials and so on). This is maintained in a ring binder (loose leaf). The information recorded is: programme reference number, visiting team, fixture detail and date of fixture and programme. This is the catalogue used when a programme is to be retrieved from the collection (assuming programmes are filed in programme number order) or to check if a programme is already in the collection. Next, the secondary check lists are updated. If a speciality is a club's home and aways, another register is kept listing all games played every season. A tick is entered against the fixture, with a single letter notation to donate programme condition (E = Excellent, G = Good, P = Poor, R = Replace at first opportunity). One-per-club-per-season programmes are recorded in a grid with teams listed on one axis and seasons along another. Either a tick or single letter notation (as above) can be used when a programme is added to a collection. Big match programmes are also recorded in a secondary catalogue, the fixture details being entered against a page devoted to each season, with again the condition notation being used. Other check lists may be maintained to reflect collecting interests – lists of British club matches in Europe, lists of friendly fixtures and so on.

The system designed is extremely time consuming, but gives a complete account of a collection and, for those with the time and inclination, will enhance the enjoyment to be obtained from the hobby of programme collecting. We are now in the age of computers and there is much that the microchip can contribute to the efficient ordering of programme collections. Computer-literate collectors can design their own databases or spreadsheets to keep track of their programmes for filing and retrieval purposes, and just as importantly for the identification of their wants. Even simpler is the purchase of a database specifically designed for programme collectors.

Eight
Comings and Goings

Pre-League

The poignancy (and perhaps even morbidity) with which a collector regards a programme from a former League club, whether now consigned to non-League football or out of business altogether, is balanced by the knowledge of successes to come when one regards a programme from a club before it was elevated to its present status. This normally means a 'pre-League' issue in the hobby's parlance, but it need not be confined to that. Wimbledon programmes from the (old) Third and Fourth Division less than a generation ago are no less fascinating than their Southern League issues a few years earlier, when one considers the sustained success enjoyed by that club in recent years. The Dons had a variety of programme styles in their pre-League days: conventional, rather boring A5 issues of eight or sixteen pages, with text, statistics and advertisements in equal measure; pocket-sized programmes in the mid-1960s and, latterly, some budget-production home-duplicated interiors with pre-printed static pages, including the cover. All of these types were characterised by blue print on white paper.

Every League club was 'non-League' at some time, but for the older members of the English football fraternity, nineteenth-century pre-League programmes are extremely rare and very valuable. Newton Heath (now Manchester United) and Ardwick (Manchester City) programmes are known to exist, but in such numbers that they would fetch thousands of pounds at auction were they ever to come to market.

In comparison, pre-League programmes from those clubs who joined the Football League in the early 1920s, when the Third Divisions North and South were incorporated, are slightly more plentiful. Carlisle United were regular issuers, favouring pocket-sized twelve-page issues printed black on white paper for their North Eastern League matches in the early 1920s.

Southern League programmes from a number of present day clubs appear on the market from time to time. Ipswich Town were comparative latecomers to the League, joining in 1938, and their Southern League programmes were printed in reasonable quantities. The four clubs admitted to the League in 1950, namely Gillingham, Scunthorpe United, Shrewsbury Town and Colchester United, all issued in the brief period between the end of the Second World War and their elevation. These issues are now scarce and would fetch hefty offers at auction.

The interest in the programme for Colchester United *v.* Torquay United Reserves, on 13 November 1948 in the Southern League, was certainly not in the bland cover, only partially rescued by an advert for a company who were 'stockists of cooking, heating and boiling stoves'. The real interest in this uninteresting programme is in the fixture status. The second elevens of the South Western clubs, Torquay, Exeter and Plymouth Argyle, all had spells in the Southern League, and while the standard of football may have been commendable, one had to wonder about the travelling involved. Torquay to Colchester in 1948 would not have been a quick day trip! Colchester have, of course, spoiled the uniqueness of this kind of programme by suffering a recent spell back in non-League football, but this is a very collectable issue – there aren't many of them around and of course it is also of great interest to collectors of the visiting club.

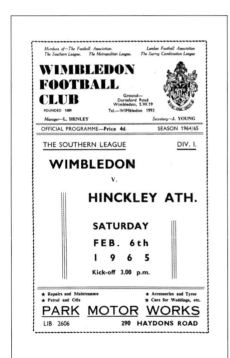

Left: *A Southern League fixture between Wimbledon and Hinckley Athletic in February 1965.* Right: *Pre-League Carlisle United issued a pocket-sized programme for an FA Cup fourth qualifying round match against Stalybridge Celtic.*

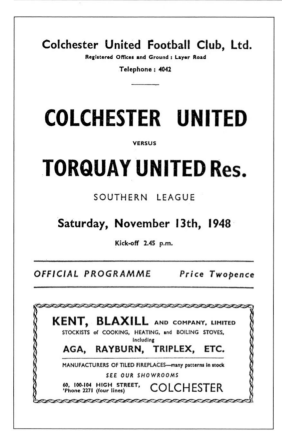

Colchester United Football Club, Ltd.
Registered Offices and Ground : Layer Road
Telephone : 4042

COLCHESTER UNITED

VERSUS

TORQUAY UNITED Res.

SOUTHERN LEAGUE

Saturday, November 13th, 1948

Kick-off 2.45 p.m.

OFFICIAL PROGRAMME   *Price Twopence*

KENT, BLAXILL AND COMPANY, LIMITED
STOCKISTS of COOKING, HEATING, and BOILING STOVES,
including
AGA, RAYBURN, TRIPLEX, ETC.
MANUFACTURERS OF TILED FIREPLACES—many patterns in stock
SEE OUR SHOWROOMS
60, 100-104 HIGH STREET,   COLCHESTER
'Phone 2271 (four lines)

A very dull cover indeed for this pre-League Colchester United match, a Southern League fixture against Torquay United reserves in 1948.

Peterborough United, who replaced Gateshead in 1960, were a very prominent Midland League club, who enjoyed frequent and high profile FA Cup success, and their pre-League programmes from the late 1950s are fairly common and may be obtained at around twice the normal price for League programmes of that age **(38)**. A little more difficult to obtain are those from Oxford United, who are more likely to appear as Headington United, the name used by the club until a year before they joined the League. Their typical non-League issues of the late 1950s and early '60s have considerable charm, given the previous name and subsequent success enjoyed by the club. For the December 1949 visit of Gravesend and Northfleet in the Southern League, Headington issued a twelve-page A5 issue, printed entirely in black on amber paper. Contents of the 4d programme were restricted to club notes, team selections, fixtures and results for their three teams, Southern League and Metropolitan League tables, supporters' club notes and information regarding forthcoming fixtures.

Cambridge United left non-League football with a high-profile friendly match against Chelsea on 1 May 1970 – and confused programme collectors for years to come by issuing two programmes for the match, arranged as part of the transfer of Ian Hutchinson. The more common programme features a photograph of the player and a shield on the cover, along with the (expensive) price of 2/-. Printing throughout the A5 sixteen-page issue was orange and blue on white gloss. Internal pages included a full-page action shot from the FA Cup final featuring Chelsea, a 'Welcome to the Abbey Stadium' feature, an article on 'Fifty Years of Progress' and another proclaiming 'We Support Cambridge United' by the Supporters' Club secretary, team groups and pen pictures of the home side, centre fold team lists, Chelsea pen pictures and team group, 'From Rags to Riches, the story of United Pools', 'Cambridge United – Ready for League Football?', an action shot of Hutchinson, a photograph of Cambridge United (the two-year-old colt owned by a syndicate of United directors) and on the back page a full-page photograph of Hutchinson. There was plenty to read and no advertising – all in all a good 'special' programme for the time **(39)**.

The second match programme was only twelve pages, printed entirely black on white gloss paper in the standard home programme format for Cambridge United in the Southern League. Fixture details and an action shot were on the cover, the editorial ran into three pages, each one topped and tailed by adverts. There was a centre spread of team line-ups in 2-3-5 formation (again surrounded by adverts), a list of United scorers, results and fixtures and a League table. In short, it was a typically brief and advert-ridden non-League programme, albeit produced on superior quality paper.

The only similarities in the programmes – both printed by Foister and Jagg Ltd of Abbey Walk, Cambridge – are the incorporation of most of the page three welcome and one

The United referred to here were Headington, later to be Oxford, in pre-League days in the Southern League.

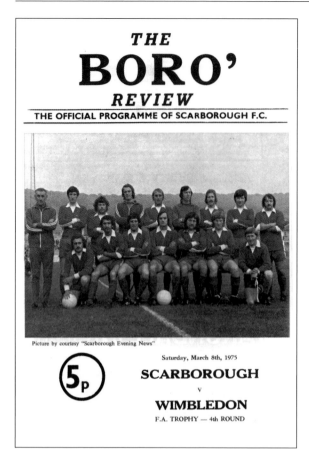

THE
BORO'
REVIEW
THE OFFICIAL PROGRAMME OF SCARBOROUGH F.C.

Picture by courtesy "Scarborough Evening News"

Saturday, March 8th, 1975

(5p)

SCARBOROUGH
v
WIMBLEDON

F.A. TROPHY — 4th ROUND

Two future League members met in the fourth round of the FA Trophy on 8 March 1975, Scarborough and Wimbledon.

of the later articles in the souvenir issue, in the running editorial of the standard production. Even the team line-ups are different, albeit only in one position – Alan Hudson is listed at No. 8 in the souvenir issue, Tommy Baldwin in the 6d standard – and the former lists a substitute for each team while the latter does not. There is a change of referee too. It would appear that the two-colour production was sold in the shops of the city as a fund-raiser in advance of the fixture, while the club went ahead as normal with their standard matchday programme.

Wycombe Wanderers were a very prominent non-League side for many decades before they joined the League, and when they entertained Oxford City in the Isthmian League on Boxing Day 1972, they issued an attractive and informative sixteen-page programme, printed in dark blue on light blue paper, with spot colour green on the front cover **(45)**.

Occasionally, you may come across a programme for a match between two pre-League sides, such as the FA Trophy fourth round tie between Scarborough and Wimbledon in March 1975. The Boro' issued their normal, tidy, twelve-page A5 programme (for 5p), containing a lengthy editorial, pen pictures of the visitors and two pages of statistics.

All of the clubs who have joined the League over the last twenty-five years were, not surprisingly, prominent and successful non-League sides, and their pre-League programmes are fairly readily obtainable, at around double normal League issue prices. High-profile cup-ties involving these clubs (Hereford United *v.* Newcastle United, Wycombe Wanderers *v.* Middlesbrough, Leeds United *v.* Wimbledon) can also be obtained by sifting through dealers' catalogues and they provide a fascinating reminder of life as a successful non-League club.

It says much for the pioneering spirit of the Football League that they were keen to expand their membership into the more remote regions of the country, although life was always a struggle for the likes of Gateshead/South Shields, Barrow and Workington. The item featured is a pre-League Workington programme for a match at Borough Park on Boxing Day 1946 against Eppleton in the North Eastern Football League. The Reds certainly did not gain membership to the expanded Football League a year later on the basis of their programme, for this is a rudimentary issue, with perfunctory club notes and the usual wide range of local advertising. By tradition, the 3d cover price was largely justified by the centre fold team lines – which were more likely to indicate the day's players than selections in today's programmes – and the Lucky Programme Number (with the winner to receive two grandstand tickets for the next match). This was issue 12 of the 1949/50 season. A pre-League, League and ex-League Workington mini-collection would be a nice part of any larger general programme collection.

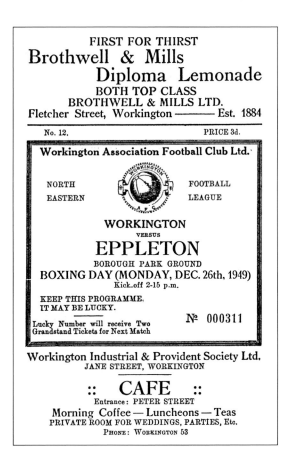

Pre-League Workington from Boxing Day 1946.

There is no better medium than a club programme for evoking memories of the way things were for football in general, and a specific club in particular, during years gone by, and this is perhaps best illustrated in the field of non-League programmes of current members of the Premiership and Nationwide Leagues.

First and last

Collectors of the programmes issued by clubs in their last season of membership of the Football League invariably feel like spectres at the feast. The last League programme before failing to be re-elected, or resigning from the League in financial ruin, is hardly a celebratory document. Far happier are the first League match programmes issued by clubs who replace the departed. Both types are extremely collectable as well as being of some football historical significance. In general, programmes throughout the first or last season of League clubs are of greater interest to collectors, and therefore more valuable, than ordinary League issues. As we have stated repeatedly, football programmes are the best recording annals of the varying and conflicting fortunes of football clubs.

Taking the dear departed first, one has to have a great deal of luck – and deep pockets – to be in possession of pre-war issues from Thames, Merthyr, Aberdare and so forth. They

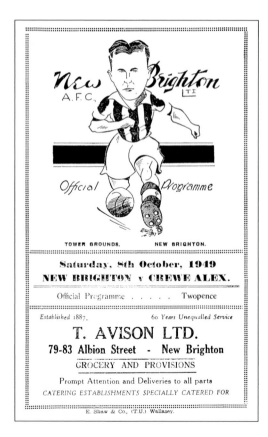

New Brighton were in their penultimate season as a League club when they played Crewe Alexandra in October 1949.

Gateshead's last home match as a Football League club against Walsall on Monday 25 April 1960.

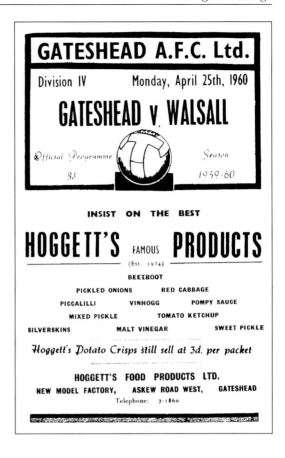

do exist – but in single numbers only, some seventy years after their clubs drew their last League breath. Merthyr Town issued a four-page (A4 folded sheet) 1d programme for the visit of Crystal Palace in the Third Division (South) on 2 May 1927. Space was obviously at a premium, with the front cover being used for the editorial, 'While You Wait' by 'Pennydarren' (which also happens to be the name of the ground). The inside pages were team lines surrounded by advertisements and the back page was filled entirely by adverts, so 'Pennydarren' had the only word in this light brown coloured programme.

First to fall after the war were New Brighton, who were replaced by Workington in 1951, and their red and white, eight-page issues still appear on the market, fetching offers in excess of £30.

Gateshead and Accrington were next to leave the League and remain reasonably plentiful, although home programmes now appear only on offer – which in any case they may warrant by their age, irrespective of their significance in terms of League membership. Accrington issues were never the hardest to come by in the 1950s and have survived well. They were reasonably substantial items of twenty or twenty-four pages – albeit completely dominated by advertisements and their smaller red and white issues from their last season, 1961/62, are now greatly in demand. Gateshead programmes were smaller in page number, but often printed on superior quality paper, so they too have survived the passing decades. Limited in content, the black-on-white productions were occasionally brightened by the use of spot colour on the front-page design.

Further northern clubs fell at the end of the 1960s and early '70s – Bradford Park Avenue, Barrow, Southport and Workington. Their home programmes remain reasonably plentiful and are sold at roughly double the value of contemporary League programmes. Collectors have been sweeping up these issues in recent years and their value will certainly appreciate in the near future, as demand for them continues. While the dwindling home support for these ex-League clubs will collect fewer programmes as they suffer non-League football, new generations of collectors of the League teams they played maintain the demand.

For more than a decade, there were no new instances of last season League programmes, despite annual scare stories about the perilous financial position of lowly clubs. Eventually, however, Aldershot and Maidstone United succumbed. The introduction of promotion and relegation from and to the Conference also increased the collecting set. Darlington, Colchester United and Lincoln City fell, happily to return after only one season; Halifax Town took longer to return while Scarborough, Hereford and Doncaster await their resurrection.

Only the legislators have saved Torquay United, Northampton Town and Exeter City in recent seasons, although doubts about their ability to beat the drop result in a disproportionate interest in their current season programmes from collectors anxious to steal a march – and beat the increased prices – on other last season collectors.

Up to the time of writing, there has been a considerable resurgence of interest in this category of collecting, with recent movements between the Conference and Division Three. Some collectors actively seek last season in the Conference for a promoted club, or the first season in it for a relegated club. One of the great tantalising aspects of football programme collecting is a question like – will the Maidstone United issues of 1992/93 (their last season in the League) be as sought after in fifty years time as those of New Brighton are today? With the happier side of first and last collections (the first programmes of clubs newly elected, or promoted, to the Football League), passing mention should be made of expensive and rare pre-war issues. The formation of Division Three saw more than forty clubs admitted to the League in the early 1920s. All immediately issued regular programmes, if they hadn't before, and these are now extremely valuable, by virtue of their age and scarcity, more than seventy years on.

It is strange to note, looking today at an honours list which includes FA Cup, League Championship and European trophy victories, that Ipswich Town entered the League as comparatively recently as 1938. They were prolific issuers in their brief Southern League days and continued that into the League, where a number of copies of their first match programmes against Southend United on 27 August 1938 exist and occasionally surface on offers lists. The thin paper and awkward large page size of pre-war Ipswich programmes means that comparatively few have survived, which is a shame because the twenty-four-page issue is particularly attractive, with a black and white background to the heading on the front page and the footballer in blue and white.

Aldershot, who joined the Football League in 1932, issued a twelve-page A5 programme in their last season in the Southern League. The internal eight pages were printed black on poor quality white paper, each page having a column of text or statistics, alongside a column of small adverts. The outer cover was printed dark blue with red spot colour on a better quality of white paper **(37)**.

First season League programmes of Oxford United, who replaced Accrington Stanley in 1962, and Peterborough United, who replaced Gateshead in 1960, sell at a premium in dealers' catalogues. Much more plentiful are the first season programmes of Wigan Athletic, Hereford United and Cambridge United. These can usually be obtained on straight-forward sale, although a sharp-eyed and knowledgeable dealer may double the price to £1 or more in recognition of the first season status. More valuable – and potential offers items – are the first match in League programmes of these clubs.

In the late 1980s and early '90s, there were a number of clubs who gained promotion to the Football League by virtue of winning the Conference; Wycombe Wanderers, Barnet, Scarborough and Maidenhead United all entered by this means and their first home programmes (and opening away match, if that came first) are all now sought-after by collectors of this set, either being purchased for a multiple of their cover prices, or sometimes appearing on offers lists. Maidenhead's League tenure was short-lived and their programmes are now quite collectable. Colchester United, Lincoln City and Darlington went out of the League and came back into it again, thanks to the Conference, and the keenest of collectors would include their first match back programmes in their collecting wants.

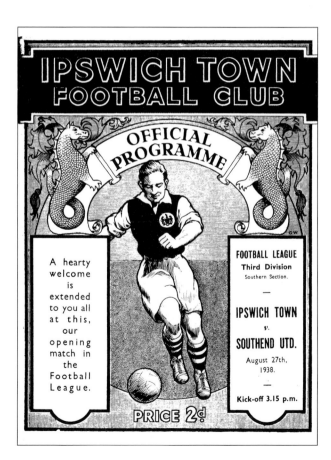

Ipswich Town's first programme in the Football League on 27 August 1938.

Many of the League's newcomers have been high achievers – Wimbledon being the most notable, while Oxford United have been League Cup winners. It is fascinating to look back to their first season programmes to reflect on the progress they have made in their comparatively short careers as League clubs.

As a guide to what to look out for as far as first and last League season programmes are concerned, here is a checklist:

Last season in League

Accrington Stanley 1961/62, resigned mid-season
Aldershot 1991/92, expelled mid-season
Barrow 1971/72, to Northern Premier League
Bradford Park Avenue 1969/70, to Northern Premier League
Chester City 1999/2000, to Conference
Colchester United 1989/90, to Conference
Darlington 1988/89, to Conference
Doncaster Rovers 1997/98, to Conference
Gateshead 1959/60, to non-League
Halifax Town 1992/93, to Conference
Hereford United 1996/97, to Conference
Lincoln City 1986/87, to Conference
Maidstone United 1992/93, resigned August 1992
New Brighton 1950/51, to non-League
Newport County 1987/88, subsequently non-League
Scarborough 1998/99, to Conference
Southport 1977/78, to Northern Premier League
Workington 1976/77, to Northern Premier League

First season in League

Barnet 1991/92
Cambridge United 1970/71
Cheltenham Town 1999/2000
Colchester United 1950/51
Colchester United 1992/93 (returned from Conference)
Darlington 1990/91 (returned from Conference)
Gillingham 1950/51
Halifax Town 1998/99 (returned from Conference)
Hereford United 1972/73
Kidderminster Harriers 2000/01
Lincoln City 1988/89 (returned from Conference)
Macclesfield Town 1997/98

Maidstone United 1989/90
Oxford United 1962/63
Peterborough United 1960/61
Scarborough 1987/88
Scunthorpe United 1950/51
Shrewsbury Town 1950/51
Wigan Athletic 1978/79
Wimbledon 1977/78
Workington 1951/52
Wycombe Wanderers 1993/94

First and last need not apply only to matches of clubs coming into and out of the League. Those with an interest in football history may wish to collect programmes from League debuts and last games of famous footballers. Since the Heysel, Bradford and Hillsborough tragedies, there has been a greater emphasis placed by clubs on their stadia, leading to a succession of new grounds being developed.

Ground openings and closures mean one thing to programme collectors – commemorative programmes to be obtained. The 1997/98 season alone saw the opening of four new grounds in England and that meant the closure of the same number at the end of the previous season.

The accepted norm for such commemorative matches appears to be the production of an A4 sized brochure. That's what Sunderland did for the visit of Liverpool on 13 May 1997 to play a special match to mark the last game at Roker Park. Team pools were on the inside front cover, a programme of events was on page four and the season was rounded up with two pages of club news and a further two-page picture spread of the last League game at the old ground, against Everton **(40)**.

There are features on the grounds at which Chris Waddle has been based in his illustrious career, articles on two young Sunderland players Richard Ord and Allan Johnston and a three-page diary of the season followed by two pages of statistics. The remainder of the forty-eight pages is a pure wallow in nostalgia, recalling the Roker Park years. This is a beautiful and fitting programme, which provides outstanding value at £2.50.

Stoke City issued a brochure-style programme to mark their farewell to the Victoria Ground and they commemorated the opening of the Britannia Stadium with a forty-four-page brochure for the League match against Swindon Town on 30 August 1997. There are many references to the new stadium and its facilities, and a two-page picture spread of its construction, but the majority of the features are common to the standard Stoke issue of that season, presented in a large-page format complete with high gloss card cover; the cover price was £3 **(41)**.

Bolton Wanderers did Burnden Park proud with a massive seventy-two-page brochure for its last match, against Charlton Athletic in the League, on 25 April 1997 **(42)**. In common with other special occasions which doubled as League matches, there are the standard features of visitors coverage, previous matches, season's statistics and so on. However, by far the bulk of the programme is a celebration of the club's 102 years at Burnden Park, brilliantly compiled and illustrated with features and interviews of many players and officials with

Souvenir Programme of
OPENING MATCH
AT THE
NEW ROOTS HALL GROUND
VICTORIA AVENUE, PRITTLEWELL
SATURDAY, 20th AUGUST, 1955
at 3.15 p.m.

Photograph by C. W. Bruce   By kind permission of B.K.S. Charter Air Service

FOOTBALL LEAGUE, DIVISION III (SOUTH)
SOUTHEND UNITED
VERSUS
NORWICH CITY

PRICE
SIXPENCE

The first match at Roots Hall featured Southend United versus Norwich City on 20 August 1955 in the Third Division (South).

memories of the old ground. This was beautifully produced in full colour with a laminated light card cover and was excellent value at £5.

Four months later, Bolton were celebrating the opening of the Reebok Stadium with a Premiership match against Everton on 1 September. A similar production, this time of sixty pages, was issued with extensive coverage of the construction of the stadium, and many pages on the facilities available at the new ground (which would, in other circumstances, be counted as advertising!). The remaining features are expanded versions of what became the normal Bolton League match programme that season, with perhaps more pictorial coverage permitted by the number of pages. The cover price was £4 **(43)**. The fourth club to open a new stadium in 1997/98 was Derby County.

A number of clubs moved grounds in the 1940s and 1950s, and programmes from the first games at Boothferry Park (Hull City), (Port) Vale Park and Southend United's Roots Hall are interesting items. Norwich City were the first team to visit Victoria Avenue, Prittlewell, on 20 August 1955, and United made a special effort with their A5-sized programme, increased number of pages, better quality paper and a different (if not particularly special) cover to their contemporary League issues.

No longer with us

There is no sadder sight in a programme collection than an issue from a defunct club when it was hale and hearty – and probably in membership of the Football League. Even in the years leading up to a club's liquidation, or failure to obtain re-election, there is never any hint in the text of their match programme that disaster is just around the corner. In earlier programmes, there may even be justified celebration of some success.

Bradford Park Avenue, for instance, who failed to gain re-election to the Football League in 1970 and who subsequently went out of business altogether, played host to the Czechoslovakian national team in the early 1960s, Southport won the Fourth Division Championship in 1972 (only six years before they were unceremoniously ejected from the League) **(44)**, while Accrington Stanley were very much at the forefront of early floodlit friendlies in the 1950s, oblivious to their ignominious resignation from the League in 1961. Perhaps most notably, Newport County advanced to the quarter-finals of the European Cup Winners Cup only a few years before losing their League status in 1988.

These programmes are fascinating and enduring relics from a previous footballing era, if a little morbid. The subsequent fate of the clubs involved mean that the programmes are important historical documents. Collectors with a keen eye on football history may extend this subject to include clubs from other countries (Third Lanark in Scotland, Belfast Celtic in Northern Ireland, St James' Gate, Transport and any number of Cork clubs in Eire), or from other grades of football. A collection including League issues from clubs such as Gateshead, Barrow, Workington and Southport would not be complete without subsequent issues as non-League clubs.

There are also, sadly, any number of examples of exclusively non-League programme producers who are no longer with us. Scrutiny of the list of FA Amateur Cup winners reveals names of defunct clubs such as Pegasus and Ilford & Leytonstone, whilst Corinthians and Casuals have since amalgamated. Others, such as Bishop Auckland, Crook Town and Harwich & Parkeston, would be unlikely national trophy winners today. There are many other instances of famous old non-League clubs no longer in existence. Any number from the Romford area (including the club of that name), Leamington, Guildford City and Bedford Town have all disappeared. Programmes from all of these clubs may still be picked up by close scrutiny of dealers' catalogues, or some assiduous rummaging at programme fairs. For those with a real passion for minutiae, there are hundreds, if not thousands, of instances of non-League clubs who have changed their names, through amalgamation, ground moves or simply for the sake of a fresh image.

The major component of these collections, and the most popular type, are ex-League club programmes, and issues from those clubs who have lost their League status in the last three decades may still be picked up for £2 or less, albeit around twice the price of standard League issues of the same era.

Gateshead, for example, were 1d penny programme producers in the years immediately before the Second World War. The black print on very poor quality white paper issue is reminiscent of near neighbours Newcastle United's programmes of the 1930s and '40s, although the printer from Laygate, South Shields, would suggest a strictly local arrangement. Gateshead, whether under that name or in their South Shields persona, were never issuers

Saturday, Jan. 29th. **No. 28.** *Price One Penny*

GATESHEAD
OFFICIAL PROGRAMME
A.F.C.

Well worthy of support!

Newcastle
BLUE STAR
ALES

BRITAIN'S BEST BEERS
Brewed by
THE NEWCASTLE BREWERIES, LTD.

A pre-war ex-League issue. Not many 1937/38 Gateshead programmes have survived the passing decades.

of large programmes. Even in their last days in the late 1950s and early '60s, their programmes were slim affairs, and this one amounted to only eight pages, hence the 1d price tag. Issue number 28, produced for the match played on 29 January, would suggest the existence of reserve issues, and one can only guess at the scarcity of these items – as this is a very rare pre-war, ex-League item indeed. This particular programme was for a match against Hartlepools United in 1937/38 and pride of place in the advert-laden issue goes to Newcastle Breweries Ltd, identifiably part of Scottish & Newcastle Breweries today.

Barrow were notable for producing highly readable programmes with unchanging, somewhat boring, covers which only latterly included match details. Indeed, right up until the club lost its League status in the early 1970s, the Holker Street programme was one of the most absorbing and value-for-money productions in the land. Even for a Lancashire Senior Cup-tie programme against Manchester City on 3 January 1955, the Holker Street club issued a full twelve-page programme and it was an example of one of the best provincial programmes of that decade. The cover featured the impressive club crest, price and an advertisement scarcely changed in two decades. It was entirely blue on white gloss paper, while the internal pages were printed in black on white gloss. The brief welcome on page three was followed by a quiz, cartoon, Barrow scorers and the last visit of City on page four;

there was a substantial 'News and Views from Holker Street' on page five, two major articles on the first two pages after the centrefold team lines and an inside back page fixture list.

In Scotland, the most notable of the ex-League clubs was Third Lanark, whose last season was 1966/67, but who last issued programmes in their final First Division season of 1964/65. The distinctive red and white, twelve-page programmes now sell for around £5, although their age is beginning to see them confined to offers catalogues. Long before the demise of Thirds, Edinburgh lost three League clubs. Edinburgh City did not make it into the 1940s, St Bernards played their last game in 1942 and only Leith Athletic managed to limp into post-war football.

St Bernards were prolific programme issuers in the late 1920s, through the 1930s and even in their last few seasons as members of the wartime North Eastern League. Their programmes changed little over the years: eight pages, printed black on thin white paper, with advertisements dominating a limited amount of text and club information. Needless to say, they only appear on offers lists now and cost upwards of £70.

On 15 September 1947, Rangers visited Old Meadowbank in Edinburgh to play Leith Athletic and officially opened the reconstructed ground, which had been requisitioned by the British Army during the hostilities of the Second World War. Derequisitioning was finally arranged to allow the club to return for season 1947/48 and their elevation into the old

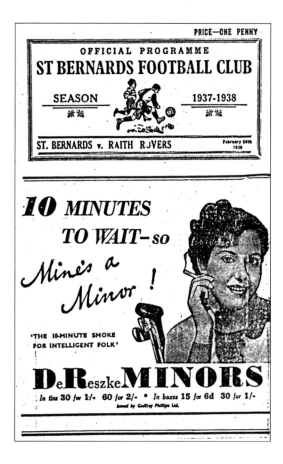

You have to search for the St Bernards name above a very dominant cover advertisement in this February 1938 programme.

Scottish League Division B. In the previous season they had been languishing in the old C Division, which was primarily composed of the reserve elevens of various Scottish League clubs. Sadly, the club failed to live up to the hopes outlined in the programme's narrative and eventually fell out of the Scottish League and were officially wound up during the mid-1950s.

The programme issued for the Rangers fixture was an eight-page publication, slightly smaller than A5 size, in black print on white semi-gloss paper. The first page had the club and match details, page two consisted entirely of the club's 1947/48 fixtures, pages three through to six had a narrative entitled 'Random Reflections', basically outlining a short history of the club and their future intentions, with team line-ups and a team photograph of each club printed at the top of pages three, four and five. The final two pages were taken up with full-page advertisements, one for a firm of gentlemen's tailors and the other for the old Edinburgh based and published *Evening Dispatch* newspaper. The issue is fairly basic as programmes go, but is one of the very few produced by a club that had to live in the shadow of the more prosperous and better supported Hibernian FC. Because Rangers were the visitors it does put it into the much sought-after category, and this despite the fact that the Glasgow club played what was virtually their reserve eleven. The programme was printed by George C. Mackay Ltd, Leith, Edinburgh.

A special programme issued by Leith Athletic to reopen their Old Meadowbank ground in September 1947.

London pride in the early 1960s

Earlier in the book, we saw how Chelsea and Arsenal were beacons of light in the gloom of general programme awfulness in the 1950s. As clubs throughout the country failed to improve their programmes when the Swinging Sixties got underway, it was London which once again provided the shining exceptions to the rule of mediocrity.

Chelsea continued to produce an excellent programme and they were joined by West Ham United. Both favoured a small-page format, shorter than the then-standard A5 size, but larger than the mini pocket-sized issues of the late 1950s and early '60s. Arsenal and Tottenham Hotspur also favoured this page size and, while their issues were amongst the best in the country, they were more predictable and short of the extra ingredient which set the Stamford Bridge and Boleyn Ground programmes above the herd.

The Hammer was lovingly tended by Jack Heliar, whose family printing firm had presided over the West Ham programme from its birth. The editorial was affectionate and thoughtful, and information on the club and its staff was imparted in a manner which made readers feel involved and informed. The editor's lifelong involvement with the club lent a historic perspective, both in terms of recollections and in commentaries on the modern game. However, the West Ham programme was no one-man band: managers, coaches, players and – in deference to the new pop society – the matchday disk jockey and announcer all contributed to a lively, yet exceedingly homely, programme. Completely devoid of advertisements (in common with its counterparts at the other major London clubs), *The Hammer* was also first to introduce full-colour photographs of players **(46)**. Across the capital, the good work of the previous two decades was being continued at Stamford Bridge. The redoubtable Albert Sewell edited a compact twenty-page programme which brimmed with club information. There was good pictorial coverage of previous matches, features on past and present players and a complete statistical and factual account of playing affairs at first team, reserve and youth level.

Part of the attraction of these programmes, looking back some thirty-five years, is that each one had its own identity: local printers, editors who were usually long-standing supporters, and content which reflected the pre-commercialised days of 1960s football meant that no two club programmes were alike. The small-sized Chelsea, West Ham, Spurs and Arsenal programmes of the early 1960s may not take as long to read as their 1990s descendents, but they retain a charm and character that the modern emporia of colour and gloss cannot hope to reproduce.

After the World Cup

Football enjoyed a renaissance following England's 1966 World Cup victory. Spectators flocked back to the grounds and a number of individuals fed off the new air of confidence and began to try out some new ideas. Foremost in this was Jimmy Hill, who transformed Coventry City from a struggling lower League club into a First Division outfit which (to date) has retained its place in the top flight.

The matchday programme was one of a number of areas of the club that Hill transformed and modernised. The Coventry issue was turned from a conventional A5-sized, rather boring, traditional programme into *The Sky Blue*, a glossy, large and multi-page extravaganza of photographs and features. It was in tune with the modern era, resembling the new magazines which were appearing on the bookstalls (one of which, of course, was *Jimmy Hill's Football Weekly*).

It wasn't all for show – at one-shilling it was the most expensive in the League, reflecting high production costs, and it was the first to hit the 10p price tag after decimalisation, so it was as much a commercial enterprise as an image builder. It was undoubtedly value for money, however, and the pioneering Coventry City matchday magazine encouraged other clubs to take a long, hard, critical look at their own programmes **(47)**.

Midlands neighbours Wolverhampton Wanderers quickly followed suit. Wolves traditionally had one of the better programmes of the 1950s and early '60s, but they had become jaded and predictable, and they followed the Coventry example with relish. *Molinews* was launched as a large-page production, filled with features and photographs. Ironically, the return to large-page productions set the clock back to pre-war days, when many clubs favoured this size. Indeed, Spurs retained that format up to and including their double-winning season in 1960/61, only as a four-page folded sheet issue.

This splendid Wolves programme was ahead of its time in October 1968.

ALBION NEWS

Volume 61 Number 18 Official Matchday Magazine 1/-

Albion v Crystal Palace
Football League Division 1
The Hawthorns
Kick-off 3pm Saturday, Jan 10/70

This West Brom programme from 1969/70 introduced modern artwork and design to football programmes.

Still in the Midlands, West Bromwich Albion took the development a stage further. They enlisted the help of graphic designers – an unheard of notion in football programmes – who produced the first designer programme. To emphasise the radical step, they turned the programme on its side, making it landscape rather than portrait. Page make-up was unrecognisable from traditional programmes and photographs were manipulated to create a design image. Content, too, was much improved, giving programme buyers a good return for their (inevitably) higher cover price. Once the home of the Industrial Revolution, the Midlands thus initiated the programme revolution, the consequences of which we see before us thirty years later. The inertia and complacency of decades was swept aside and programmes have continued their development to this day.

League Cup finals

The Cinderella competition may have ultimately become a beautiful princess, with Wembley finals and automatic qualification for the UEFA Cup, but it is still something of an afterthought where programme collecting is concerned. Club collectors will of course include these programmes as part of the season's haul, but for someone not wishing the full committment of collecting every home or away in both league and cup competitions, a collection of League Cup-ties would be a manageable and fascinating sub-set. The timescale straddles four decades so far, providing the thrill of the chase in tracking down some of the early 1960s programmes, the contrast in styles of the 1970s and the rather more easily obtainable programmes of the last twenty years. Concentrating on the later issues initially would allow a substantial collection to be built with relative ease and at modest cost.

One of the fascinations of cup-tie collections is the departure from run-of-the-mill League opposition, particularly in early rounds. There is not the occasional joust with non-League opposition as in the FA Cup, but the seeded nature of the first couple of rounds in recent years has guaranteed the visit of the giants of the English game to lower division teams (and vice-versa in the reverse legs). This gives the opportunity for both clubs to depart from their normal League programme styles; the small club to contemplate a larger, souvenir programme and the top division club to perhaps economise on style and price with a smaller edition of their normal matchday magazine.

One of the most interesting big match collections involves League Cup finals, which provide a variety of issues – and competing teams – over the forty years of the competition. There have also been five changes in the tournament's name, reflecting the sponsorship of the Milk Marketing Board, Littlewoods, Rumbelows, Coca-Cola and now Worthington. Major clubs, many of them newly engaged in European club competitions, gave the tournament a wide birth in its early years. Thus, we find Aston Villa and Rotherham United contesting the first final in 1961 over two legs and the programmes from both games are much sought-after and now quite valuable.

The following season, it was Norwich City *v.* Rochdale, and while there was great local interest in these matches, the attendances (and hence the programme print runs) were modest in modern terms. For the second leg, Rochdale issued one of their pocket-sized programmes of the period. Twelve glossy internal pages are finished with a stiff cardboard cover in yellow and black, and the contents are split between normal editorial, with the addition of team photographs of both sides, and advertisements. This is an extremely rare programme now, with collectors wishing to complete the 'set' of League Cup finals having to pay over £100, but when a copy does appear on the market, it is invariably in excellent condition, due to its size and cover.

The two-legged final format continued for another four years and resulted in League Cup final programmes being produced by Birmingham City, Aston Villa (again), Leicester City (twice), Stoke City, Chelsea, West Brom and West Ham. While some of these programmes are more plentiful than others, they remain extremely collectable and fetch prices well in excess of contemporary League issues.

The Football League, in an effort to secure the involvement of the major clubs who had been reluctant to enter the early League Cup competitions, changed the final tie to a single match, staged at Wembley, with a place in the Fairs Cup (later UEFA Cup) for a First Division winner. Queen's Park Rangers beat West Brom in the first Wembley final in 1967 and the big match programme was produced in an old-fashioned A5 format, to suit the size of the inserted issue of *Football League Review*, the organising body's weekly magazine which was distributed via clubs' matchday programmes (**48**).

Almost as an aside, there are usual programme spin-offs when so-called smaller clubs have an unexpected trophy success. A week after winning the League Cup, Queen's Park Rangers entertained Peterborough United in a Third Division fixture and issued a twelve-

The rarest and most notable of the mini-programmes, Rochdale versus Norwich City, League Cup final in 1961/62.

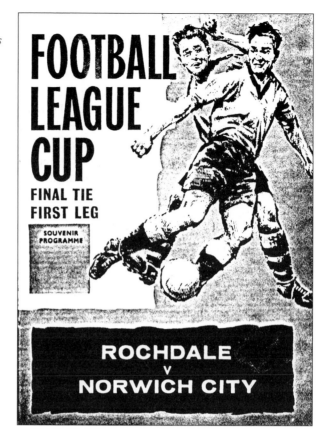

page 'Wembley Souvenir Issue'. This was an advertisement-free production (apart from an invitation to tear out one page as an application for a 1967/68 season ticket) which contained reflections and photographs of Rangers' big day. The small-sized format for League Cup finals was used for a number of years until the *Review*, and its successor *League Football*, ceased publication, whereupon more conventional big-match sized programmes were published. The preference for brochure (A4) big match programmes, usually with laminated covers, was adopted for League Cup finals from the mid-1980s. The cover price, needless to say, increased accordingly.

One of the most attractive features of this category of programme for collectors is that a number of so-called 'lesser' clubs have known unaccustomed success in this fixture. A collection of League Cup finals will mark the unique success of clubs such as QPR, Swindon Town, Stoke City, Norwich City, Oxford United and Luton Town within national competition. A much prized item in any Stoke City fan's possession is the programme for the 1972 final against Chelsea, when the Potters won their first (and so far only) major trophy. With sixteen large-size pages, with full colour photographs throughout, the A5-sized *Football League Review* was incongruously stapled into the centre (**49**).

Followers of the major clubs, meanwhile, will take comfort in the more regular successes of Arsenal, Manchester United, Liverpool, Spurs, *et al*. There have been numerous replays

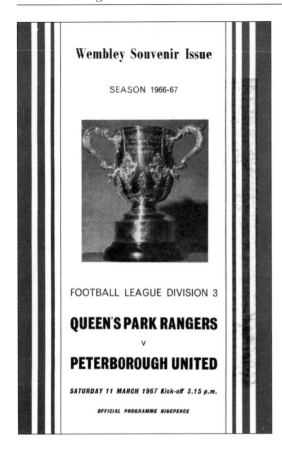

The special programme issued by Third Division QPR to celebrate winning the Football League Cup in 1967.

required, however, and these have taken place 'in the provinces', leading to further varied and collectable programmes. Unlike the FA Cup, semi-finals are played over two legs at the contesting clubs' grounds and these issues are interesting to collect, particularly on a current season basis when the games are invariably televised live. As with most categories of programmes, this set can be collected to suit any budget. While final programmes from the early years of the competition now fetch huge sums, those from the last twenty-five years can invariably be picked up for a pound or so each, providing younger collectors with the opportunity to collect an attractive set at prices they can afford.

Modern European finals

Domestic cup competition finals come around every year, but a British club's involvement in a European club competition final is sufficiently novel to make the occasion very special, if not unique, in the memories of that club's supporters. For historical significance, therefore, a collection of European final programmes is very worth while accumulating.

There is also something of a challenge involved, as issues from foreign shores are a little bit more difficult to obtain than programmes from, say, Wembley or Hampden. A dealer's transport costs may inflate the price, although at least in view of the progressively more expensive domestic final programmes, European items may not suffer in comparison. The supply line to the UK may prove to be erratic and there are occasions when more than one programme is on sale at the match, particularly in countries and cities where 'ground issues' of programmes are commonplace.

A final in Munich's Olympic Stadium will undoubtedly see an issue of *Die Blaue*, alongside the official UEFA version. Rome would see *Roma Mia* produced and there are many other instances of this – there were two different programmes produced for the European Cup Winners Cup finals contested by Rangers in 1967 and Aberdeen in 1983. In the past, there have been finals for which no programmes have been produced – Moscow Dynamo *v.* Rangers in Barcelona in 1972, Feyenoord *v.* Celtic in Milan in 1970 and the Bayern Munich *v.* Atletico Madrid replay in 1974 – and the Ajax *v.* Juventus issue from Belgrade in 1973 is so rare that it was thought for some years that no programme was published. It is most unlikely that such a scenario would be repeated today, with UEFA particularly programme-conscious, in line with their committment to championship sponsors and advertisers.

Further spice is added by collecting UEFA Cup final programmes, which are published by the host clubs, these games being played on a two-legged basis. Many make a special effort for such an auspicious occasion – some, and this includes English clubs, have issued versions of their domestic programmes. Leeds United's issues for their home Fairs Cup finals against Dynamo Zagreb in 1967 and Ferencvaros a year later were little different from their normal League productions; the Arsenal programme for their final against Anderlecht in 1970 was indistinguishable from their normal 1969/70 issue, while Liverpool made few changes to their normal *Anfield Review* for the visits of Borussia Moenchengladbach in 1973 and Brugge three years later in UEFA Cup finals.

Newcastle United adopted a colourful cover design for most of their Inter Cities Fairs Cup-ties in the late 1960s. The rather ordinary League programme of the time was enhanced both in appearance and the number of pages, with a particular effort made for the Fairs Cup final against Ujpest Dozsa from Hungary on 29 May 1969. A message from the Newcastle chairman, a welcome to the visitors in their own language and three pages of pen pictures and head and shoulders photographs took the twenty-page programme to the centrefold teams. In the second half of the issue, results to date in that season's competition, action shots from the semi-final, a manager's page and head and shoulders photographs of Newcastle's scorers in the competition that season mixed with some local advertisements (**50**).

The UEFA Cup, formerly the Fairs Cup and before that the Inter Cities Fairs Cup, had a somewhat unusual birth. Birmingham City were prominent in early finals and once again normal domestic issues were produced for matches against Barcelona in 1960 and AS Roma a year later. A London select contested the first competition, played over two years, and home matches were played at Stamford Bridge, White Hart Lane, Highbury and Wembley, producing interesting and collectable programmes.

Nine

In Modern Times

The modernisation of programmes in the 1970s

With the post-1966 World Cup boom beginning to fade, football entered the 1970s realising that modern marketing and commercial techniques would have to be applied to the sport to enable it to compete with the growing number of alternative pastimes and leisure pursuits. This brought about a radical transformation in the role and format of matchday programmes, coincidental with the first sponsored football tournaments.

Initially, these took the form of brand new competitions – as opposed to sponsors attaching their names to established tournaments – and so the Watney Cup was born in England, followed shortly afterwards by the Dryborough Cup in Scotland. To link the countries, and Ireland (both north and south), the Texaco Cup was established. Suddenly, more and different programmes were being made available for collectors. European ties had been added to the normal domestic staple diet in the fifteen years since 1955 and now came additional tournaments and inter-country fixtures, such as Wolves *v.* Derry City, Airdrie *v.* Ballymena United, Motherwell *v.* Spurs and St Johnstone *v.* Ipswich.

The brewers Watney broke new ground with programmes for their pre-season tournaments, which were in stylised form and published on behalf of the sponsors, rather than the home club. Sixteen A5 pages in size, the tournament sponsors were the only advertisers, so there was plenty of room for features on both teams, the tournament and the television personalities involved in ITV's coverage of the competition (**51**).

In Scotland, a year later, Dryborough's launched their pre-season tournament, although programmes early in the competition were distinguished only by having a sponsor's cover round the normal host club programme – and a number of them didn't issue. Special programmes were issued for the finals, such as the sixteen-page, A5-sized 5p production for the 1972 final at Hampden between Celtic and Hibernian. As over the border, the restriction of advertising to the tournament sponsors provided more room than usual for features on the teams and tournament (**52**).

For their competition, Texaco provided a common style of outer pages for their tournament programmes, although the host club was left to its own devices with regard to internal pages. One or two clubs, perhaps slightly pretentiously, began to call their programmes 'matchday magazines' and they were certainly increasing in size – and cover price. Gloss paper became widespread and print techniques improved with the move away from letterpress to litho, and so photographs became a better and more prominent feature. Colour began to creep in, spreading from the First Division down through the leagues as the decade progressed.

Coventry City, programme pioneers in the 1960s, continued to explore new avenues in the 1970s. They took the magazine concept quite literally by producing a very large page-size programme (even bigger than today's brochure-sized cup final issues), which featured lifestyle articles, loosely related to football, to complement the standard contents. An example of this was the back page, full-colour photograph of a glamour girl, posing chastely. It is interesting to note that few, if any, clubs followed this 'laddish' route, and certainly not in the last couple of decades.

To modern eyes, 1970s programmes look brief and inadequate, but contrast them to the issues of the previous decade and it can be seen that clubs were beginning to pay more than lip service to modern presentation and marketing techniques.

Collecting Tips: What to look out for

Throughout this book, we have sought to explain the various types of programmes that could be collected, how to obtain them, how much they might cost to accumulate and the reasons why each different set of programmes might be attractive to a football fan. There are hundreds of thousands of programmes produced in this country alone, each and every season, and with every collector's funds limited to some extent, a degree of choice or specialisation is necessary.

There are a number of collectable programmes that do not fit into the neat sub-divisions explored over the previous chapters, or which perhaps can straddle two or more categories. These are worthwhile purchasing shortly after the match, as they gain value (both in monetary and historical terms) with the passing years, and will come into their own when looked at ten or twenty years later, when they rekindle memories of a special or unique occasion – the real purpose of keeping football programmes.

The match programme is an ideal medium for commemorating special occasions in the game. Individual player's milestones, for instance, can be explained and illustrated in print and then recalled in years to come by those who retained the programme. A century of caps, breaking a goalscoring record, or an appearance record are all appropriate. Take, for instance, the Leyton

Orient v. Brighton programme when Peter Shilton became the first person to play 1,000 League games in England. Despite a larger print run, the programme sold out well before kick-off time and is now much sought-after.

There are footballing occasions when the notable event cannot be anticipated. Denis Law's six goals in the Luton Town v. Manchester City FA Cup-tie of 1961, which was abandoned with City winning 7-1, then Luton winning the rearranged fixture, makes either of the programmes an interesting addition to any collection. Record victories or defeats, record high or low attendances – all are perfectly marked by the programme for the historic fixture.

There are, of course, tragic events which attract collectors – for example, Hillsborough, Ibrox and Bradford and the commemorative matches played in their aftermath. The Munich Air Crash has led to a series of much sought-after programmes: the game immediately before the ill-fated trip, when United beat Arsenal 5-4 at Highbury, the programme from the match itself against Red Star Belgrade, which recently fetched £1,900 at Christie's football memorabilia auction, and the Manchester United v. Sheffield Wednesday programme in which the United team list was left blank.

Happier events are best commemorated by their programmes – such as a significant addition to a ground, or indeed the opening of a new stadium. More poignantly, special programmes are issued for

Red Star Belgrade versus Manchester United, February 1958 – the last match of the Busby Babes. This programme is now worth over £1,000.

the last matches at the old stadia. Those are invariably unique issues full of interesting historical features. All of these types of programmes, and many more, comprise a powerful storehouse of footballing memories, the release of which in years to come is the reward for building a collection of football programmes.

Testimonials and other benefit matches

There appears to be no middle ground with regard to the standard of programmes issued for testimonial and benefit games. They are either large brochure-type issues which swamp contemporary League items in terms of size and scope, or they are almost an afterthought, providing only a basic souvenir of the occasion.

The popular conception that the more notable the player, the larger the souvenir programme may be true today, but it was not always so. Several star internationalists who enjoyed benefit matches in the 1950s and early 1960s would obtain little recollection of the glittering tributes paid to them from the brief and inadequate programmes which marked their testimonial matches.

On the other hand, the trend of brochure-style programmes for megastars started with Stanley Matthews' big night in April 1965 and has continued to the present day. While the club on whose ground the match was played, Stoke City, were issuing twelve-small-page programmes on a Saturday, a massive 100-page brochure was issued for the fixture between a Sir Stan Matthews XI and World Stars. It sold for 2/6d at the time, compared with the 6d Saturday programme, but there was no diminution of sales as fans clamoured to mark the occasion with a substantial and authoritiative account of the 'Wizard of the Dribble's' career **(53)**.

This demand for such programmes on the night of the fixture is continued after the event. Added to those collectors of the competing clubs, and perhaps the player's other clubs, are enthusiasts who specialise in collecting testimonials and benefit match programmes irrespective of the name of the recipient or the clubs involved. Furthermore, while perhaps greater numbers were printed in anticipation of matchday demand, there would be fewer available for post-match sales, which themselves are subject to greater demand.

This speciality is of interest to those with an appreciation of notable footballers, from the loyal club men whose lengthy service is rewarded, to the superstars whose exceptional skills are being lauded. The style and content of the programmes themselves attract a certain type of collector, for they invariably provide an extensive biography (and occasionally autobiography) of the player, providing information and statistics that perhaps would not be obtained in any other publication – including, for those of a certain status, the inevitable ghosted 'autobiography'.

The Charlton brothers, Bobby (with Manchester United) and Jack (with Leeds United) had long and distinguished playing careers with their first clubs, and were rewarded with sell-out testimonial matches against Celtic. Both games were marked by unique programmes – stapled on the shorter edge, twenty-four-page glossy brochures, with plenty of colour photographs. These issues were years ahead of their

One of the earliest testimonial or benefit programmes was for Patsy Gallagher on 4 January 1932.

time (both matches were played in 1972/73 season) and were appropriate tributes to such prominent figures **(62 and 63)**.

Another great player, from an altogether different era, had a very special programme issued for his testimonial match. Patsy Gallagher was arguably the main reason Celtic dominated Scottish football in the years immediately after the First World War, and when a Celtic and Falkirk Select met a Scottish League Select at Celtic Park in January 1932, a twenty-four-page, pocket-sized programme was sold for 2d. For its time, it gave a substantial account of the player and his career, and it is now an extremely rare item.

Dealers' catalogues invariably have testimonial sections, where the fixtures are conveniently grouped, and the same applies at programme fairs. Prices vary widely, with the benefit of such fixtures being largely a phenomenon of the (late) 1960s, '70s, '80s and '90s. Collecting testimonial match programmes should not involve too many excursions into the more expensive offers sections and auctions.

A brief flirtation with newspapers

As modern printing techniques improved and marketing men got to work on the image of football, so clubs adopted the matchday magazine format for the barely recognisable glossy production that used to be called their programme. Having devoted resources to improving the quality and quantity (in terms of pages and content) of their programmes, they began to take a hard commercial look at sales figures and questioned traditional selling methods.

One obvious path was non-matchday sales, with newsagents a prime target. The traditional programme did not look good amidst magazines and newspapers on shop shelves, so a few clubs decided to radically change the format and shape of their programme. First to do so were Oldham Athletic, who after decades in the doldrums were attempting a revival under their new chairman, Ken Bates. *Boundary Bulletin* ran for two seasons (1966/67 and 1967/68) and, although printed in two colours on glossy paper, it was in (small) tabloid format. In terms of content it was immeasurably superior to standard programmes, but its short life suggested that it was not a commercial success. Next to try were Derby County, with *The Ram*. This was more enduring, lasting a decade, and started and finished as a fairly substantial tabloid newspaper, latterly with full-colour photographs. Cambridge United tried a cut-down version of Oldham's glossy 'paper' and Plymouth Argyle emulated Derby's newspaper format, although for a shorter period.

In the early 1980s, with commercial managers a fixture at almost every club, it was the fashion in football to attempt to be different – whether it be through playing-kit design, commercial activities, or the format of programmes. Added to some unusual page sizes and a choice of syndicated inserts, was an outbreak of newspaper productions. These were published on behalf of a number of clubs from all areas of the country, including Northampton Town, Preston North End, Tranmere Rovers and Walsall, but that particular fad was of even shorter duration than the earlier one and none continued into their second year.

Still with an eye to the newsagent's magazine business, a number of clubs over the years have thought about a weekly programme, irrespective of whether or not there is a home match that week. The programme format is retained, but there are no team line-ups. One of the first to try this were Motherwell in the early 1970s, with their small-size, traditional-looking programmes. Like all others since, the lack of matchday sales meant that the inter-match issues were a commercial disaster and the experiment was short-lived. Birmingham City were probably the last to try this in the early 1990s, but like all other variations on traditional matchday sales, this experiment barely lasted a season.

Inserts and supplements

Attempts at producing a syndicated football programme have arisen in many decades. In the inter-war years *The National Football Programme*, which was in effect little other than a Saturday morning football paper, sold on matchdays outside grounds. This venture had rather more success with its Scottish version, where there were fewer competing club issues, than south of the border, where fans would have had better value for money from the excellent club programmes of the time.

It was a surprise that it took so long after the war to resurrect the idea, at least in some form, and in 1965/66 *Soccer Review* first appeared as a supplement to thirty-four different clubs' programmes. This was quickly adopted by the Football League, renamed *Football League Review* and then *League Football*, and ran until December 1974, when the high cost of paper and improving standard of programmes made it uncommercial.

Many clubs eagerly included the official mouthpiece of the League's Lytham St Annes headquarters. It's full-colour finish, solid content and photographic coverage greatly enhanced many inadequate club issues and it allowed these clubs to charge 1/- for programmes which, without the insert, would have struggled to justify a cover price of 3d. It was not universally popular, but was certainly readable, and its demise in 1974 meant that a number of laggard clubs had to look seriously at improving their previously neglected programme.

Left: *'The National Football Programme' was published for over thirty years, with a number of copies of the Scottish version appearing on the market from time to time. This edition was from 17 April 1920.* Right: *The first season of the* Soccer Review *supplement to club programmes.*

The supplement went through two name changes, emerging as League Football, *firmly the mouthpiece of the Football League.*

Specialist printers began to enter the programme printing market in a big way in the early 1980s – displacing the longstanding local printers – and one of their selling points was the inclusion of syndicated inserts. These were free to clubs, provided the firms printed their programmes, with national advertising making them commercially viable. A number of clubs adopted them with relish, once again for the reason that they greatly 'padded out' an otherwise inadequate issue. *Programme Plus*, *Centrespot* and *On Target* were just three of these printer-provided inserts.

This fashion lasted barely three seasons, as the third-party publishers began to realise what has dawned on many before and since – there are no quick and easy bucks to be picked up in programme production. The most recent attempt was in the late 1990s and on reflection it is some surprise that it took so long for a competition sponsor to get involved in such a venture. The *Nationwide Review* lasted just over a season and was heavily supported by the Football League's sponsors. In content and presentation, this was more a throwback to the old *Football League Review* days, but it was regarded as even more of an irrelevance by modern programme buyers, who had quite sufficient to read in the modern, bulky programmes issued by their clubs. One suspects that the groundstaff swept up more copies on a Monday than were tucked away in programme collections.

Every now and again, a new marketing manager will float the idea of a standard programme for a sponsored League or tournament. This regular brainwave founders on past experience and the fact that if programme collectors want to read articles about other clubs, they will buy a monthly or weekly magazine at the newsagents; in their matchday programme fans want to read about their club and the fixture at hand.

Reserves and youths

Believe it or not, those single, photocopied teamsheets, or folded A4 sheets, which you receive on admission to a reserve or youth team match (or which perhaps cost you 10p) to find out who's playing will be worth more to a collector in years to come than the glossy, colourful production at first-team level.

The sheer scarcity of reserve issues is the reason for this – clubs have a good idea how many die-hards and players' relatives turn up for reserve and youth games, and run off the requisite number of programmes on their photocopiers. Post-match surpluses are practically non-existent and, such is the quality of the 'programmes', any that are left are invariably binned. Few current season collectors bother with these issues, the price of postage to obtain them far outweighing their cover price, and clubs are therefore not encouraged to overproduce for postal sales. If further proof of this disregard for 'stiffs' programmes is required, ask yourself how often you see them for sale in the club shop.

In a decade's time, however, this season's reserve match issues will assume a different importance to those collectors who have almost exhausted their first-team collection and who will look to expand into other areas concerning their beloved club. Whereas ordinary first team League and cup programmes from 1960 onwards rarely appear on offer, 1960s' reserve match issues invariably do, and 1970s' issues are more expensive than their first team equivalents.

Ironically, the situation is not quite so marked in the years leading up to the early 1950s. Crowds for reserve matches were quite large in these pre-modern travel, pre-television days and programmes were produced in good quantities – and were of a good standard, invariably of the same style as first team issues, albeit with fewer pages. If anything, these programmes fetch lower prices than their first team contemporaries.

Newcastle United issued a full blown sixteen-page programme for the visit of Liverpool Reserves in March 1939. Printed by T. & G. Allan of Newcastle in black and white, haircuts and men's clothing adverts take up the front inside cover, with team line-ups on the third page. Then come the United officials (even giving the manager's phone number), club gossip and more adverts, with Liverpool Reserves having their own page. Advertisements proclaiming A1 bikes at £3 19s 9d or 2/1- a week and the half-time scoreboard covers the centrespread, whilst football news,

Newcastle United issued full sixteen-page programmes for their reserve matches in March 1939.

more adverts and three pages of Newcastle statistics complete a very newsy and informative issue. The programme is particularly interesting because Albert Stubbins played for United Reserves before his post-war move and immense popularity at Anfield. It cost 1d and did not make mention of the gathering clouds of war, only six months away.

There are many occasions in which the contents of the programme, rather than the occasion or the rarity and antiquity of the issue, make the item special. One such example is the FA Youth Cup final between Manchester United and Wolves, played on 23 April 1954. The special issue of *United Review* was no more than a four-page, greatly reduced version of the club's standard issue, with red spot colour on the front page, joining the black-on-white, non-gloss paper of the remainder of the programme. Contents were teams (in 2-3-5), a few paragraphs on the competition, both teams' progress to the final and (mostly) pen pictures of both teams. This latter aspect carries most interest – in the United team were Colman, McGuiness, Edwards, Charlton, Pegg and Scanlon, joining Hawksworth, Beswick, Rhodes, Harrop and Littler. Wolves fielded Sidebottom, Griffiths, Harris, Bolton, Fallon, Timmins, Round, Mason, Bonson, Murray and Cooper. The cover price was an expensive 2d.

Some famous names are included in the Manchester United versus City Youth Cup semi-final from April 1964.

A few clubs incorporated reserve match details into a first team programme – notably Aston Villa and West Brom in the late 1950s and early '60s. Thus Aston Villa *v.* Manchester United in 1958/59 also includes Villa Reserves *v.* Wolves Reserves and West Brom *v.* Bolton in 1957/58 incorporates WBA *v.* Wolves in an FA Youth Cup-tie. From that era and earlier, a fair indication of the standard of reserve programmes issued by the club is whether or not they are included in the numbering sequence. A late-season Chelsea or West Ham programme numbered 35 or 42 would suggest that substantial reserve programmes were issued for the Saturdays when the first team was not at home and included in the numbering sequence of that season's volume.

For a spell in the early 1960s, Manchester United issued very attractive four-page A5 reserve match programmes, which gave good value for the 2d asking price. The front page 'banner' was a sketch which seems unusual in a United programme and it was accompanied by a first-team action photograph. Inside there was a substantial editorial of over a page, which gave a detailed background to the match, and opposite were the team line-ups (in 2-3-5 formation). The back page was taken up with pen pictures. There were no adverts, save for a mention of the shop which supplied the tannoy music at Old Trafford, and the front page had the banner in red, with the remainder of the issue black on white light gloss. This particular issue is for a FA Youth Cup semi-final against local rivals City. United included Rimmer, Fitzpatrick, Noble, Anderson, Best, Sadler and Aston, while City had Doyle and Pardoe in their side. This was excellent value for 2d and a lovely little folded sheet programme.

The lesson is a clear one – if you are considering collecting your club's programmes, obtain the current reserve and youth team programmes NOW – it will save you time and money in the future!

Friendly programmes

There are many aspects of modern football that are taken for granted which, forty or fifty years ago, were considered out of the ordinary. Improved communications and travel arrangements have led to matches against European or pan-Continental sides becoming commonplace, both at home and abroad, while the demands of television and universal use of floodlights have unlocked many more opportunities for matches.

This was not the case in the 1950s, when clubs were in the process of installing floodlights, and the 'floodlit friendly' was something of a novel attraction to supporters who knew only of 2.00 p.m. kick-offs in the winter months, and midweek evening matches which stopped in September and only started again in April. Continental sides were invited to English League grounds with increasing regularity, while there was considerable cross-border movement as Scottish clubs visited south of the border and vice-versa.

In virtually every instance, a programme was issued – sometimes a standard League issue, other times a truncated programme and often a folded or single sheet. Coincidental with the novelty value of floodlit football decreasing, the number of pre-season preparation matches played by clubs increased. From about 1970 onwards, the number of these fixtures escalated, with more lowly clubs eagerly playing host to major outfits, who in turn may send mixed sides to non-League clubs. The major clubs will also embark upon pre-season tours, often to exotic locations.

All of this has resulted in a dramatic increase in the number of programmes issued for friendly matches and introduced a new category for collectors. There are probably sufficient copies being generated for single-club collectors to amass a reasonable sub-set; there are certainly enough programmes generally for a collector to build a large and extremely varied collection.

From the glossy, full-size issues of major clubs playing other big clubs to the special programmes issued for the visit of top clubs to lesser lights, through to the cut-down League programmes as editors wearily confront a raft of extra and unwanted fixtures down to the perfunctory team sheets and folded sheets – through the leagues, across country boundaries and into the non-League scene – a variety of friendly match programmes are issued.

Dealers and club collectors may also bring back foreign tour programmes from abroad, and once again these vary from team sheets to glossy, magazine-style productions. The latter type of programme is full of advertisements and it is in the

EVERTON FOOTBALL CLUB
Official
PROGRAMME

Vol. 5   No. 12

FOOTBALL MATCH.
6 EVERTON
versus
3 ALBION ROVERS
At GOODISON PARK
WEDNESDAY, OCT. 23rd, 1946.

KICK-OFF 3-15 p.m.

PUBLISHED BY AUTHORITY OF
THE EVERTON FOOTBALL CLUB CO. LTD.   PRICE - ONE PENNY.

The unlikely pairing of Everton versus Albion Rovers was as unusual then as it is now.

interests of even the most minor of continental clubs to issue these for all matches, including the visit of British clubs pre-season, to keep their advertisers happy. Even the most obscure of pre-season tour matches, played at the height of summer in a small town or village, is likely to see a programme of some sort produced.

There is an interesting history of programme issues for British clubs on far away tours, with programmes coming back from South Africa, America, Canada, the Carribean, Asia and Australia and New Zealand all adding to the diversity of friendly match programme collecting.

In its earliest manifestation, there are some fixtures which, to modern eyes, seem incongruous. Clyde were frequent visitors to major English clubs, including Arsenal, while Partick Thistle visited Tottenham Hotspur. In 1946, Everton played host to Albion Rovers and issued a small, four-page folded sheet for an October Wednesday afternoon kick-off. Printed in blue on thin white paper, the inside pages held first team and reserves results and fixtures and opposite were the team lines, with Joe Mercer playing for Everton and Jock Stein for Albion Rovers. The back page was mostly advertising.

Schools and youth representative games

There has been no scientific investigation into what makes football supporters collect souvenirs and football programmes – and there is unlikely to be in the future – but they can probably be split into three broad categories. Firstly, there is the mild hobbyist, who just likes collecting. Secondly, there is the club fanatic, who wishes to obtain everything associated with his favourites. Thirdly, there is the football historian, who relishes the antiquity and folklore of the sport.

This third kind of collector explains why a comparatively obscure category of programme is frequently collected: that of representative matches at schools or youth level. These are certainly not collected for the quality of issue – often they are bland, abbreviated productions with little content other than the basics of match and squad information – but instead they have value in the reading of them years or decades after the fixture was played. The attraction is in the team selections and particularly in pen pictures of the players.

While there may be little interest in the glowing account of a fifteen year old's golden promise if he subsequently made no impression at all on the professional game, there is considerable fascination in reading of the future internationalist or club star in his formative years. It is also interesting to consider the various players who made up the team – some of them going on to greatness, either together in one side, or as future opponents, while the majority achieve little more than an ordinary career in the lower reaches of senior football.

Against Scotland Schools at Chesterfield in 1951, England fielded Duncan Edwards and David Pegg, both destined for Manchester United. Seven years later, for the same fixture but this time at Wembley, Terry Venables and Billy Bremner were on opposite sides. In 1959, at Derby, England fielded Chris Lawler and Martin Peters, while Peter Shilton featured in the 1965 England *v.* Scotland Schools programme at Wembley.

The range of venues used for these matches makes for a varied collection. The majority of League club grounds in England have hosted a Schools or Youth international at one time or another. This plethora of matches, virtually all of them lost in the mists of time, means that a complete collection is just about impossible. In terms of sustaining long interest in the collection, that is a good thing; on the other hand it may also be a source of great irritation and frustration to those intent upon completing sets.

Schools international fixtures, played annually at Wembley and at League grounds around the country, can be picked up for very modest sums from dealers' catalogues, or at programme fairs. While rare because of their age, programmes from either side of the Second World War may be obtained for a fraction of the cost of League, cup or senior international issues. This applies even to older items, such as the substantial sixteen-page programme for London Boys *v.* Glasgow Boys in November 1948. Printed black on white gloss paper, with a yellow and black cover, this was a more impressive issue than many FA Cup final and full international programmes of the time, and that may be explained by the prominent sponsorship of the fixture by *The Star* newspaper.

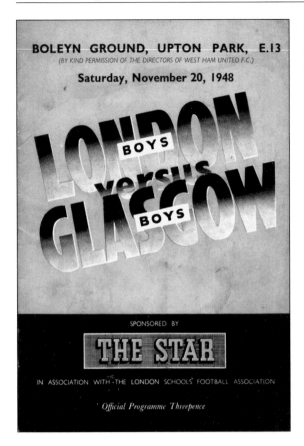

The stars of the future played in this London Boys versus Glasgow Boys match at Upton Park in November 1948.

Usually uninteresting in appearance and neglected in appeal, these programmes should not be ignored or tossed to one side before their contents are scrutinised. Their value to later generations comes with hindsight.

Under-21 internationals

The heavy defeat of England by Hungary, home and away, in the early 1950s prompted a great deal of radical thinking in this country and one of the most enduring relics of the reaction to the footballing lessons handed out by Puskas & Co. were under-age internationals. At first, the team was described as 'Colts', as with the first fixture for which a programme was produced, a 6-0 victory over Scotland at Clyde's Shawfield Stadium in February 1955.

By the time of the return match at Hillsborough a year later, the Under-23 tag had come into vogue and this continued until 1976, when the age limit for participation in these fixtures was reduced to twenty-one. Fixtures were spread around the country and responsibility for programme production invariably fell on the host club, leading to a wide variety of shapes, sizes and prices of Under-23 and Under-21 programmes.

This makes for a very varied collection, which is all the more attractive to collectors because of two additional factors. Some of these fixtures are quite hard to track down and the programmes – usually cut-down versions of the club issues of the time – may not have been printed in large quantities. It may therefore take a bit of work and research to complete the set.

Usually, such difficulties mean that the programmes are regarded as scarce and are priced accordingly, but that is not the case with these fixtures. There are sufficiently few people collecting Under-21 and Under-23 international programmes, that they can be picked up for little more than the cost of contemporary League programmes.

The other major benefit in collecting these programmes is their content. As with Youth and Schoolboy programmes, there is particular fascination in reading about the early careers of players who went on to become distinguished internationalists, and great interest in the high hopes at an early stage of those who never made the transition to full international level – players who were perhaps destined for a life in the lower leagues. The 1956 match against Scotland saw England field Jimmy Armfield (Blackpool), Duncan Edwards and David Pegg (both Manchester United) and Johnny Haynes (Fulham). Scotland included Alex Parker (Falkirk) and Alex Young (Hearts), who were later to be Championship winning team-mates at Everton.

It is now fairly rare for friendly internationals to be played at this level and it is a matter of some regret that the regular matches between the home countries have fallen by the wayside. That is because UEFA organise their Under-21 tournament to coincide with both World Cup and European Championship qualifiers, so every two years there are four or five matches at home and the same number away from home. The quality of continental programmes is very variable. Some are at least as good as those produced in this country, others are little more than team sheets. There are still some countries who are not very programme-orientated and issue no official programmes for such matches. Usually, the best that can be obtained by collectors are team sheets prepared for the media. Programmes from past matches against continental opponents test the football knowledge of collectors as they try to spot current internationalists in the opposing side.

Odd shapes and sizes

It is ironic that, given the huge diversity of shapes and sizes adopted by football programmes over the decades, that the modern era sees almost exclusive adoption of a standard (16cm x 24cm) page size, at least in the English leagues. At the one extreme, we have had tabloid newspapers masquerading as programmes and rarely a season goes by without at least one club adopting a brochure-sized production (in 1998/99 it was the turn of Bolton Wanderers and Bristol City).

For special matches, one or two clubs have issued a poster-size production folded twice to brochure dimensions and including, on one side of the sheet, recognisable programme features, with a photograph dominating the reverse. On the other hand, we have seen the tiny pocket-sized issues of the late 1950s and early '60s, and the slightly larger issues produced by Arsenal, Spurs and West Ham for much of the 1960s (and in the Hammers' case also the 1970s). Crystal Palace in the 1960s and Bristol City a decade later favoured a very narrow programme, albeit as tall as other programmes of the era.

The vast majority of British programmes have been A5 in page size (15cm x 21cm). This is a particularly convenient size for those producers with one eye on the printing budget, for it is simply an A4 sheet folded. It is very rare to find a non-League club, or a lower League club in Scotland, using anything other than this size.

Occasionally, clubs have tried to freshen their production by stapling and folding the shorter edge, producing a landscape orientation rather than the conventional portrait. One of the first to adopt this style was the pioneering West Bromwich Albion programme of the early 1970s, along with Crystal Palace a couple of years later. There have been a few isolated incidents in the following decades, notably with Hamilton Accies and Airdrie in Scotland and before that at Watford for a number of years.

The Vicarage Road club were also the most enduring users of the 'square page' format, which had a conventional height but a larger width. This was by no means unattractive and a number of clubs followed, but only briefly. In the years immediately following the Second World War, many clubs favoured eight-page programmes, arrived at by folding a long sheet twice, thereby preventing the need for collation and stapling. The majority of Scottish clubs have used this format at some time or another – notably Hearts in the 1940s and Raith Rovers, who were probably the most enduring, using the staple-less format from 1949 until 1968.

In a notoriously competitive environment, it is something of a surprise that at least one British club has not gone out of its way to produce the smallest ever programme on at least one occasion. Every now and again someone uncovers a tiny, or immense, page size from a foreign land and ponders whether there has ever been a smaller or larger programme published.

Glorious technicolour

Nowhere has the advances in modern print technology been seen in matchday programmes more than in the widespread use of full-colour printing. It is now very unusual to see a League match programme in England that does not have full colour reproduction on every page, but it is only in the last twenty years that such technicolour coverage, previously the exclusive prerogative of magazines, has spread.

The first full colour to be seen on programmes was at Wembley Stadium. The first match there, the 1923 FA Cup final between Bolton Wanderers and West Ham United, sported a full-colour cover (in design only and not in photography). For a number of years Wembley persisted with this style for FA Cup finals and England *v.* Scotland matches, the full colour sketches of the stadium, players and match action making up in glorious technicolour what they lacked in art appreciation.

The 1930s saw full colour abandoned by Wembley, to be replaced by mono- or two-tone designs, some of them in the art deco style of the period. Sketches of the stadium and match action reappeared after the war, but the colouration was, at best, three colour – usually a green background with blue and red detail, along with black print. One or two clubs came close to full colour, also featuring three colours in their cover designs. Wolves were notable in this respect, with their old gold complemented by the other colours of the club crest, whilst Banbury Spencer of the Birmingham Senior League had full-colour printing for their cover sketch in the 1958/59 season.

Full-colour photographs first appeared in club programmes in the late 1960s, initially as inserts (at West Ham) and then included on a four-page spread which was obviously printed separately from the rest of the monotone issue. The major clubs, with their huge print runs, were to the forefront of this development – notably Chelsea and Arsenal.

In the 1970s, full colour was still in its infancy, although most clubs had incorporated a number of colours in their front page design, and occasionally throughout the issue. Initially, colour was confined to the front page photograph, which sometimes changed with each issue, although more often did not for the entire season. A national advertiser was invariably on the same sheet (on the back page) thereby assisting with the considerable extra cost. The Scots were slow to embrace full colour in their club programmes and indeed the honour of the first in that country fell to lowly Albion Rovers in the late 1970s, although the cover design and background stadium scene were of little artistic merit.

Today, we take full colour photography and design very much for granted, and indeed developments in recent seasons have seen laminated card covers, and (notably with Sheffield Wednesday) partially laminated cover designs which add to the aesthetic quality and attraction of those splendid productions.

Other cup finals

The most popular single fixture for programme collectors is the FA Cup final, followed for big match collectors by League Cup finals and, in their respective countries, Irish, Scottish and Welsh Cup finals. Twenty-five years ago, FA Amateur Cup finals may have been added to the list of 'must haves' every season, although the successor FA Vase and FA Trophy competitions have not captured the imagination to the same extent, and these are now largely the prerogative of non-League collectors.

There is a great deal of poignancy attached to a collection of FA Amateur Cup finals, as many of the post-war participants are now amalgamated or defunct. Two clubs to fall upon hard times within a decade of reaching the prestigious annual event were Dagenham and Skelmersdale United, who contested the 1971 match at Wembley. Programmes for these matches were rarely inferior to FA or League Cup final issues and the substantial 10p edition is an excellent souvenir of what was once the highlight of the non-League calendar.

The big match collector can now add the Auto Windscreens Cup final (and its various predecessors), the Anglo-Italian Trophy and, from recent seasons, the Zenith Data Systems Cup. In Scotland there has been the B&Q Cup (now the Challenge

THE FOOTBALL ASSOCIATION
AMATEUR CUP COMPETITION OFFICIAL PROGRAMME 10ᵖ

versus

SKELMERSDALE UNITED

FINAL

SATURDAY 24th APRIL 1971   Kick-off 3 p.m.

EMPIRE **WEMBLEY** STADIUM

Two names you will no longer see on the fixture list – Dagenham and Skelmersdale United – when they met at Wembley in the 1971 Amateur Cup final.

Cup) and the pre-season Drybrough Cup, which followed the English example for the Watney Cup in the early 1970s. Across the borders, there have been Texaco and Anglo-Scottish Cups. All of these competitions have provided sub-sets of programmes for single club collections, but they have also widened the scope for big match collectors and, with the various changes of sponsors and tournament formats, they provide an interesting and extremely varied set in themselves.

As products of the highly commercialised last twenty years, they are also readily available and fairly cheap, being priced at £1-£2, with the occasional scarcity edging up towards the £5 mark. The Full Members Cup was inaugurated to compensate for the exclusion of English clubs from European competition. The finals of the competition from 1986, 1991 and 1992 sell for around £5, the rest for less than £2. These programmes may appear under their various sponsors names – such as the Simod Cup or Zenith Data Systems Cup.

Associate Members Cups, initially for clubs outside Divisions One and Two, and now for Nationwide League clubs, have final programmes priced between £2 and £4, as do the Anglo-Italian Cup final programmes. The former competition may also appear as the Freight Rover, Sherpa Van, Autoglass, Leyland Daf or Auto Windscreens trophy. The comparatively modest price fetched by these final programmes extends back almost thirty years, with the 1970 Derby *v.* Manchester United Watney Cup final fetching little more than £4, 1971 West Brom *v.* Colchester £2 and 1972 Stoke *v.* Hull City £3.

The majority of these finals will be a mere footnote in the history of the game, but for some of the participating clubs they represent an unaccustomed share of the spotlight, and perhaps a rare visit to Wembley Stadium. Because of this, their programmes are interesting, varied and collectable.

Ten
Do You Want To Know More?

A quick guide to football programme prices

There are two constant subjects of dispute amongst football programme collectors: condition and price – the latter is very often determined by the former. The value of programmes is constantly changing with the passage of time and changes in collecting trends. There is, therefore, little merit in producing a comprehensive price guide within this publication – it would be out of date just weeks after going to print! However, there is a regularly updated booklet giving lists of prices that you might be expected to pay. The justification for this pamphlet (priced £1 plus postage, or five first-class stamps, from Programme Monthly, PO Box 3236, Norwich, NR7 7BE) was that it would provide some guidelines on the approximate worth of programmes to three types of reader: those with no knowledge of the current market who wished to dispose of programmes in their possession, new collectors who needed some idea of what they may expect to pay and a quick reference for collectors. The guide is compiled by scrutinising the catalogues of four of Britain's top dealers and then giving two columns of prices – the highest and the lowest that the collector may expect to pay.

There is often a great disparity between the 'low' and the 'high' quoted in the price guide. All this proves is that it pays to shop around and obtain as many dealers' catalogues (and therefore as much information) as you can before parting with your hard-earned cash. There were no patterns of pricing which emerged from the research – no one dealer was more expensive than another in general terms. There may be dealers who claim to always charge less, but be aware that they are likely to be part-time (nothing wrong with that) and will consequently provide a reduced service and carry less stock than a full-time dealer, who relies on his profits from programme trading to pay his overheads and make a wage for living. The prices are only guidelines – each seller will have his own view of the worth of a programme, based on stocks held, price paid and so on.

Wanting to sell?

If you are selling to a dealer, the price you will receive is substantially lower (by as much as 50 per cent in some cases) than the retail prices shown in their sales catalogue. Where prices are low (less than £3), the programme is commonplace and the dealer is likely to have many copies of that programme and will probably not want to buy another copy from you!

As stated above, all programme prices are subject to condition and the prices quoted are usually for clean, intact and unblemished copies with, in the case of older items, no significant faults. Just because a programme is old (over thirty years of age as a rule of thumb), this will not necessarily make it attractive to a buyer. Condition, type of fixture and comparative rarity will have to be taken into account, and only some big match programmes now achieve high prices. Otherwise, a programme will have to be forty-five to fifty years old before it will be attractive to a buyer purely on account of its age – and even then condition will remain a factor.

In general, programmes dated from 1966 onwards are very commonplace and of unexceptional worth. There may be individual items that are scarce but, with only a few very isolated exceptions, normal League and cup programmes from 1966 onwards are worth very little to dealers. Of more interest to collectors – and therefore worth a little more – are items such as representative games, friendlies, cup finals and semi-finals, testimonials, reserve and youth fixtures, European matches and local cup-ties.

From around 1955 to 1965, ordinary League and Cup programmes will be sold for little more than catalogue prices, which were as follows at January 2000 (some dealers' prices may vary by up to £1 per season):

1946/47	£10.00	1956/57	£ 2.50	1966/67	£ 1.00		
1947/48	£ 9.00	1957/58	£ 2.50	1967/68	£ 1.00		
1948/49	£ 8.00	1958/59	£ 2.00	1968/69	£ 75p		
1949/50	£ 7.00	1959/60	£ 2.00	1969/70	£ 75p		
1950/51	£ 6.00	1960/61	£ 2.00	1970/71 to			
1951/52	£ 5.50	1961/62	£ 2.00	1984/85	£ 50p		
1952/53	£ 5.00	1962/63	£ 1.50	1985/86	£ 60p		
1953/54	£ 4.50	1963/64	£ 1.50	1986/87	£ 70p		
1954/55	£ 4.00	1964/65	£ 1.25	1987/88 to			
1955/56	£ 3.00	1965/66	£ 1.25	date	Face value		

There are two main ways of selling your programmes. You may contact a dealer who will quote a price for your entire stock if he is interested in purchasing. He will want details of what it comprises – either a full list of items, or a concise and accurate summary, such as: 50 Manchester United 1950-1955, 100 Manchester City 1953-1958, 150 Manchester United 1956-1965 and so on. Some indication as to condition should be given – are there written team changes, have items been repaired by Sellotape, are parts missing (photographs or tokens cut out), are there punch-holes? The dealer may arrange to inspect the stock. It is best to obtain more than one quotation.

Alternatively, you may wish to sell the programmes yourself and this can be done through a specialist magazine. You could make up your own sales list and ask respondents to send you a stamped-addressed envelope for you to send the list to them. This would involve the most amount of work, but for the highest potential returns. Alternatively, you could advertise the best items for sale or offer in the magazine itself. It is best to obtain a copy of such a magazine to see the kind of advertisement required – this publication will also carry advertisements from dealers who will buy your programmes.

The novice to the hobby of programme collecting

Always read a dealer's advertisement carefully – for example, if he or she wants four first-class stamps for a catalogue, that is what you should send, because bulky catalogues are expensive to print and post.

Rarer programmes are usually sold by postal auction and are known as 'offers'. You write to the seller, stating clearly the programme and your bid price, with your letter to arrive before the seller's stated closing date. If you are successful, some days later the seller will ask you to send the appropriate remittance, to include return postage, and once he has received this he will send the programme(s) to you. If the condition of the programme is not as you were led to believe by the advertised description, you should return the programme(s) immediately and ask for a full refund. Keep a copy of all correspondence.

The prices in the guide may give you some help in deciding what to bid, as will the 'minimum offer' stated by the seller. If you are very keen to obtain a programme, you will bid higher than the catalogue price or standard League price for the age of the item; if you are more indifferent, you may wish to bid at around, or lower, than the catalogue price – it is surprising how many times this will be a successful method of obtaining less rare programmes which are (perhaps mistakenly) placed 'on offer'.

New collectors will obtain the majority of their early programmes at straight sale catalogue prices. When ordering from dealers, simply follow the instructions on their catalogues, remembering to include in your remittance an adequate sum for return postage. Do not be frightened to ask advice from fellow collectors or dealers – ours is a friendly and co-operative hobby.

An excellent place to discover more about programme collecting is at a programme fair. These are held throughout the year around the country, usually on Sundays between 11.00 a.m. and 4.00 p.m.

THE MODERN MAGAZINE

What once passed for a matchday programme at an early League match, cup-tie, or even a cup final, now barely serves as a team sheet at a reserve or youth game. The best modern programmes could compare with any magazine on a newsagent's shelf, such is the extent of development over a century of programme production.

It is greatly to the credit of clubs, associations and programme producers that there is universal approval for the improvements they have made over the decades; there may be the occasional complaint at having to pay £1.50 or £2 or more on a matchday, but there is acknowledgement that the bulky, colourful and glossy magazine represents excellent value for money.

Clubs now appreciate the value of a good matchday magazine. Not only is it profitable, but it acts as an unsurpassed vehicle for disseminating information to supporters. Increasingly, it is also used as a sales catalogue for the club's growing portfolio of commercial activities. At all times, however, there is the realisation that if the reader is not given value for money, then the product will not be purchased.

Thus we have an unsurpassed array of features, articles, statistics and photographs, making full use of the unique access that is afforded to the matchday magazine production team. Interviews and features on players, managers and officials are provided which could not be dreamt of by a newspaper or magazine, and these are given more space and depth than the outside media could contemplate.

An army of amateur historians throughout the country are delighted to research and write on their beloved club's history, providing authoritative information to supporters, and many talented feature writers happily contribute to their club's programme. As our major clubs get larger and players become even more remote from the paying public, the pages of the matchday programme serve an important purpose in keeping fans informed about their favourites. Some clubs continue to devote a number of features to their supporters, although the bounds of propriety and the football rulebook give the growing array of fanzines an unanswerable advantage in the publication of more trenchant views. With each passing year, programme buyers are being given more, with better quality, in their matchday purchase, albeit at a steadily higher price.

Every season, an enterprising editor or publisher uses a new idea, design or printing technique that further enhances a issue which previously seemed incapable of improvement; that idea is then developed and adapted by other clubs in the following seasons, and by that process the general standard of programme production is lifted even further.

Season after season, we continue to enjoy the highest ever standards in the long and varied history of matchday programmes.

DO YOU WANT TO KNOW MORE ?

The hobby of football programme collecting is enormous in its scope – there are thousands of programmes issued, at every level of the game, every week, around the world over the decades, and you will see that it is impossible for this book to comprehensively cover the entire subject. Increasingly, other football collectables – books, tickets, postcards, cigarette and trade cards, first day postal covers and a myriad of other memorabilia – are becoming popular and are regularly traded, so football memorabilia collecting is not just confined to matchday programmes.

The best source of information on the hobby, features on programmes through the years and various news and views which enable a collector to keep up to date with the goings on is the magazine *Programme Monthly and Football Collectable*.

This was first published in February 1981, and over the intervening years and more than 230 monthly editions, it has covered the hobby in great detail. A complete collection of back numbers forms a comprehensive encyclopaedia of football programme and memorabilia collecting. The magazine started out as 32 pages in size and recent issues amount to 140 pages so, to date, there have been roughly 20,000 pages devoted to the hobby. Copies of all back issues remain available, either in original or reproduction form (some of them greatly discounted in price) along with a comprehensive index of contents. Attractive binders are available for storing the magazine.

Half of each edition comprises advertisements from dealers, auction houses, publishers, service companies and collectors, in which programmes, memorabilia and services are for sale, exchange and wanted. Catalogue-issuing dealers are prominent advertisers, providing collectors with information about how they may find additional programmes for their collections. Up to two pages each month are devoted to listing programme fairs and auctions throughout the country, and there are reviews and adertisements of the latest innovations to enter the hobby – computer databases for collectors to catalogue and control their collections, CD-ROM collections of programmes, internet websites and so on.

The magazine also organises and publishes the annual Programme of the Year Awards in England and Scotland. A series of collectors' booklets have been published by the magazine: *Collecting Football Programmes: An Introduction to a Great Hobby*; *What to Collect*; *Football Programmes Down the Years* and a *Quick Guide to Football Programme Prices*. In the mid-1980s a series of handbooks detailing programmes issued in specific seasons in England, Scotland and non-League football were published.

Programme Monthly also runs the UK Programme Collectors Club, membership of which is free. Members may purchase a register of members, giving full contact details and collecting specialities. The magazine also acts as a voice for collectors, printing letters, opinions and requests for information or advice.

In short, *Programme Monthly & Football Collectable* magazine is the one-stop shop and ongoing work of reference for everything that is happening in the hobby and trade. The current edition is available, priced £1.80 plus 50p postage (or nine unused first-class stamps) from Programme Monthly, PO Box 3236, Norwich, NR7 7BE. Full details of advertising and subscription rates are given in each edition of the magazine.